KISS the RAT RACE GOOD-BYE

KISS the RAT RACE GOOD-BYE

A step-by-step program that
shows how you can get
your finances in shape <u>now</u>
to be financially independent
in 10 to 15 years

ELIZABETH   LEWIN,   CFP

PHAROS BOOKS
A SCRIPPS HOWARD COMPANY
NEW YORK

Library of Congress Cataloging-in-Publication Data
Lewin, Elizabeth.
Kiss the rat race good-bye : a step-by-step program that
shows how you can get your finances in shape now to be
financially independent in 10 to 15 years / Elizabeth Lewin.
    p.   cm
Includes index.
ISBN 0-88687-669-9
1. Finance, Personal.   2. Financial security.   3. Retirement
income—Planning.   4. Saving and investment.   I. Title.
HG179.L478   1992
332.024'01—dc20   92-8522   CIP

Printed in the United States of America

Pharos Books are available at special discounts on bulk
purchases for sales promotions, premiums, fundraising, or
educational use. For details, contact the Special Sales
Department, Pharos Books, 200 Park Avenue, New York,
NY 10166.

Jacket design and interior design
by Janet Tingey

Pharos Books
A Scripps Howard Company
200 Park Avenue
New York, NY 10166

10 9 8 7 6 5 4 3 2 1

THIS BOOK IS IN LOVING MEMORY OF

Michael J. Brody
more affectionately known as "Uncle Mike"
1934–1990

AND

John C. Keaveney
1938–1991

ACKNOWLEDGMENTS

My special appreciation to Bernard Ryan, Jr., whose contribution made this all possible; Richard C. Fulljames, F.S.A., Wyatt and Company, Stamford, CT, who helped with illustrations and graphs, and Budd S. Schwartz who checked and rechecked all the numbers and whose knowledge and suggestions were greatly appreciated.

I would also like to thank Helen Axel, The Conference Board, New York, NY; Jean E. Campbell, Hewitt Associates, Lincolnshire, IL: Myron I. Dworken, Dworken, Hillman, LaMorte & Sterczala, P.C., Bridgeport, CT; Robert Fajardo, Nathan & Lewis Associates, Inc., New York, NY; Ilise Gold, Gold & Roberts, Westport, CT; Sybil Gruner, Corporate Eldercare Assistance, Inc., New York, NY; Jeff Klein, Hewitt Associates, Rowayton, CT; Linda Nash, Buck Consultants, Secaucus, NJ; Douglas Tormey, Towers Perrin, New York, NY; James Waters, Towers Perrin, Saddlebrook, NJ; Henry M. Wallfesh, Retirement Advisers Inc., New York, NY, and to all the people who shared their stories with me.

CONTENTS

CHAPTER 1

Here Today . . . Where Tomorrow?

"You have reached Magic by Miller. I have disappeared for a moment. Since I am a magician and not a mind reader, please leave your name, message, and phone number, and I'll return your call when I reappear."

Danny Miller had a good full-time job in middle management. But one evening a friend dragged him to an adult education course on magic at his local high school. One session, and he was bitten by the magic bug. It brought to life something he had suppressed since he was a young teenager—the urge to be a comedian. From then on, keeping his mind on his work was a chore. "My body was just going through the motions," he says. "My mind was on magic."

For two years, Danny took one course on magic after another. He read everything about magic that he could get his hands on. He joined all the magic societies for miles around. At the same time, he kept on working full-time at his company.

But magic was gnawing at him. He was nowhere near retirement age. But for two years he had been thinking about magic and getting out of the rat race. Finally, his wife, who was a teacher, said, "C'mon, Danny. You know you won't be happy till you do it. So do it." So he told his boss what he was up to. And he knew his pension would be available in five years.

Next thing he knew, he had his first booking to perform magic for an audience—a sales meeting at his own company, at five hundred dollars plus expenses. In a short time, he built a reputation as a magician who could adapt his act to fit sales meetings, conventions, business conferences of any kind. Today he works for another company, but on a part-time, flexible arrangement, while, as he puts it, "My magic comes first."

How many Dannys are out there? Thousands. And thousands upon thousands. For instance:

- A fashion designer who sells his business, then sets up a fruit-and-vegetable stand.
- A director of marketing and communications for a large hospital who goes back to school and becomes a marriage counselor.
- A geologist who buys a country inn.
- Husband-and-wife Wall Street traders who raise ostriches.
- A nurse who becomes a crackerjack seller of pharmaceuticals to doctors and hospitals.
- A pharmacist who is taking courses at a culinary institute in his spare time.
- A flight attendant whose adult education courses include food, flora, and fauna—all for future freedom from flying.
- A former Washington banker and his wife, a former interior designer, who run a four-star country restaurant.
- A high-school guidance counselor who has become a landscape architect.
- A computer programmer in her late twenties who has turned to floral design.

How many people do you know who put aside dreams to pursue a "safe" career? How many do you know who have realized how unhappy their parents were in their careers and often heard them say, "If only I could have done . . ."

What would you rather be doing—*now*?

The Stormy Business Climate

The business climate of the 1990s tells you—indeed, is *shouting* at you—to think about what you would rather be doing. Getting ready for whatever else you would rather be doing is not only a good offense in your career game plan, it is an even better defense. The kaleidoscope of mergers, acquisitions, corporate restructuring, and tightening profit margins of recent years has been forcing one company after another—across all the fields of business and industry—to cut back on staffs. Those who have been there longest and who are paid the most are often the first to go, regardless of age discrimination laws.

What has happened is that the age of "I work for the company, the company will take care of me" has come to an end. Loyalty to the big company, and top-notch performance for it, are no longer a guarantee that you will have a job until you are 65.

Think of it this way: Whereas in the 1970s and 1980s, or even earlier, you may have thought of yourself as climbing steadily on the company ladder—moving upward with increasing responsibility for the same employer over many years—in the nineties you will need to sell your ability to any company that needs it. The ladder will be gone. Higher and higher titles will not exist. You may work for anywhere from 5 to 10 different companies, never moving upward as far as titles go, taking with you to each company, as they are needed, the portable skills you have developed.

Today, titles are out and skills are in. It is no longer a question of who you are but of what you can do. Loyalty is also out. Creativity, variety, change, and flexibility are in.

New Key Word: Self

With titles out and skills in, a new vocabulary is emerging. *Corporate gridlock, migrant managers and professionals, portable skills, self-management, portfolio of skills, marketable experiences*—these describe not who you are, by title, but what you can do. Among all the words in the new vocabulary, the most important for you is *self*.

Company management these days is encouraging that word *self*. It asks you to take on greater responsibility for your own future—for your own ability to bring to the job skills that can make the company successful, and for your own financial security. Gone are the days when working for a company entitled you to a lifelong career with secure benefits.

Toward Two Kinds of Self-Management

Think of self-management in two ways. Financial self-management is the first. Most companies now, for example, provide pension plans, some of which depend largely on the contributions the employee makes. They offer guidance through the maze of plans you can use, encouraging you to understand them and appreciate their values. They provide a wealth of programs and tools that help, from booklets, newsletters, and videos to financial planning seminars, individual financial counseling, and even interactive software programs that can give you ready access to your own personalized financial information.

The second is career self-management. Most companies do more than encourage you to take courses regularly that can help you to broaden your responsibilities or handle more responsible jobs. Most insist that you have such training. They put the responsibility for your career growth, and for your maintaining and improving your skills, right on your shoulders. They want you adaptable. And they want you not only eager to learn but willing to take training and, in fact, go find training if they don't offer it.

All of which raises questions related to why you are reading this book. What interests you? What are you good at? What skills do you have to acquire that go hand in hand with your interests?

At the same time, what is your philosophy? Are you thinking back to basics? Are you fed up with the fast track—with the seven-day work weeks, the 12- or 15-hour workdays, the big credit-card debts, the borrowing, the consumerism? Are you disturbed by the numbers of friends laid off, the collapse of banks, the decrease in real estate values? Are you ready for a more meaningful family life? Are you ready for what is being called "The We Decade"?

All of that mixed background—the changes in the way corporations are looking at you, the changes in the way you are looking at your life—may very well add up to a strong desire on your part to kiss the rat race good-bye. Maybe it means starting a new business within the career path you chose some time ago. Maybe it means a big change—a whole new career, involving some learning or training or a geographic move. Maybe it means turning your personal interests and hobbies into a money-making skill or profession. Maybe it means simply knowing you will have time to enjoy smelling the roses and listening to the birds sing. Maybe it means early retirement, literally.

Whatever it is, think of it as a beginning, not an end. And think of working at it—working to get to that goal. Whatever your dream—to perform magic, run a bed-and-breakfast, operate a photo studio—you can achieve it if you start to plan it and work toward it *today*. Working toward your big change may involve taking adult education courses at the high school. It may even call for going to see a career counselor to get an objective viewpoint on your skills and your needs, but it does *not* call for procrastination. Remember the old saw, "We don't plan to fail, we just fail to plan."

Why have others kissed the rat race good-bye? For as many reasons as there are people. Let's meet a few.

From Teaching Russian to Throwing Pots: Building a Business to Leave the Rat Race Behind

A friend loaned Ken, who taught Russian in a high school, his potter's wheel. Two years later, Ken and his wife, Shelley, who was also a teacher, were selling his creations at crafts fairs. Using Shelley's business and marketing skills, they developed his hobby into a profitable business. At the same time, they concentrated on planning for the day when Ken could step out of the classroom for good. Within 10 years, by the time he was 50, they had each managed to build up enough pension money so he could leave teaching and they could work together in their pottery.

Running their own business gave them time to pursue other interests. They put Ken's fine arts and pottery background together with his fluency in Russian to give them nine months in Russia with the United States Information Agency, as Ken set up and worked a design show that traveled through three of the Soviet republics. He was paid a salary, with a per diem allowance, while Shelley worked in the USIA office preparing the staff's expense vouchers.

Regrets? "Not a one," says Ken. And Shelley adds, "It's so wonderful to be free."

A Husband and Wife Who Started to Plan in Their Thirties

Nora was a legal secretary. Howie was a manufacturers' rep selling costume jewelry and handbags. They had lost several friends who were only in their late thirties, and both wanted out as soon as their last child finished college, when they would both be in their mid- to late forties.

Not having the advantages of corporate pension plans, Nora and Howie put together a well-disciplined plan of their own, starting when they were still in their thirties. "We saved at least 10 percent of both our salaries," says Howie. "We had just about no debt— only our mortgage. And both of the kids went to the state university, so we kept the college cost way down."

Two Who Sold Rat-Race Businesses to Gain Financial Independence

When he was 32, Lloyd found a way to merge his career as a fashion designer with his love of rock 'n' roll music: He introduced his spring collection not in the usual runway show, but in a video called

"I Keep Looking at You." It featured a song he had written, which was released on a single by Epic Records. The commercial slant gave both customers and salespeople his guidance on how the designer likes his clothing to be worn. He followed up by unveiling his next collection with another video, "We Keep Pumping."

Knowing he would burn out fast in the fashion industry, he planned to make what he could and then sell the business. Within six years, he was out. To start an entirely new career, he and his brother visited the Hunts Point produce market in the Bronx, where most of the fruit and vegetables destined for stores in New York City and suburbs are distributed, and studied the business. Then he found a suburban town in Connecticut that needed a new produce stand. He set one up, and the customers keep coming in.

Frank is another who sold a business to gain financial independence. With a graphic arts background, he found himself working in the credit department of a large corporation. Two years later, having learned all he could, he joined another member of the department in going out to open their own collection agency. The business was highly successful. He figured he would keep it for 10 to 15 years. That would be enough of that cold-blooded business. But when his younger brother was killed in an auto accident, Frank decided to sell out—at age 37. He got about $180,000 for it and, with the money invested, plus his wife's income, he went back into graphics and at the same time began to write. Small graphics jobs came in. A few stories were published. Neither brought much money. And both were lonely occupations.

Frank decided to develop a business that got him out of the house. His father and his brothers were in the construction business, and as a child he had learned how to fix things. "So I put an ad in the local papers offering my services as a handyman. That's somebody there's a tremendous need for. If the float in the toilet needs to be replaced, I can do it for a fraction of what a plumber charges. And the phone never stops ringing. Now I get my business from word of mouth. By the time I go into somebody's house, they have a list a mile long of little odd jobs that need doing. If it weren't for me, those jobs probably wouldn't get done. And I do as much or as little as I feel like, so I have time for the drawing board and the writing."

These are only a handful of the stories told by Americans who have found ways to kiss the rat race good-bye toward the end of the twentieth century. The moral in every case is, "Happy endings follow smart beginnings."

The impossible dream? No. It has been achieved by others. You can achieve it, too. But you must work at it and plan for it, and you cannot work for it and plan for it unless you understand all the elements that make it possible. It is a matter of rethinking your financial strategies, and managing your financial life as carefully as you have been managing your career. The purpose of this book is to help you do that rethinking and managing.

The impossible dream? No. Not if you start planning for it with your next paycheck.

Throughout this book, you will meet other people who have kissed the rat race goodbye. At the end, we will meet in depth Ken and Shelley, and Howie and Nora, who have already started new careers, as well as Judy, a single woman of 33 who is planning to be financially independent within 15 years, and see just how they made their dreams come true.

CHAPTER 2

Life Begins at . . .

Since you are reading this book, you probably already have a long-term goal: to gain financial independence for yourself, so you don't have to work for anyone if you don't want to. That may mean any one of more than thousands of possibilities—from working at your own pace in arts and crafts as a painter or photographer or woodworker to starting up your own business or consulting firm in the line of business you already know so well . . . from fishing in river or deep-sea waters to smacking a golf ball at least 18 holes a day . . . from growing roses or apples or house plants to baking cheesecakes or refinishing furniture or restoring old cars . . . from traveling to see the world or your grandchildren to giving your time as a volunteer at the hospital or library or schoolhouse.

All such possibilities have one thing in common as you look ahead: They are goals. To achieve any one of them, you know you must devise a plan. Woodworking needs tools and a shop. Photography demands a darkroom. Golf calls for living close to if not right alongside a golf course. A full-time culinary hobby invites a larger kitchen, with professional stove and oven and pots and pans.

All these are life-style goals. They may involve adding to your house or moving to another part of the country. Planning to reach them calls for financial goals. You would not set out to do any one of them, today or in the future, if you could not afford to. "Oh well," you may say, "that's 10 or 20 years in the future. I don't know what I'll want to be doing. I just know I'll want out of the rat race by then."

Exactly. *Being able to do any one of them, or to do nothing at all, calls for financial goals.* A financial goal is easy to define: You accumulate money. The goal may be short-term or long-term. It may aim for an amount of money that is relatively large or small compared to other financial aspects of your life. But the goal is simple: It is money saved—put away. Or, to state it in another way, the goal is capital.

Goals—financial or otherwise—are useless if they are not realistic and attainable. If you decided to go on a diet, you know it would be unrealistic to try to lose 10 pounds in 10 days. But you know that if you set two months as the goal for taking off 10 pounds, and if you find 4 or 5 pounds gone at the end of the first month, you have set a realistic and attainable goal—and you find yourself pleased, proud, unfrustrated, and thinner.

Goals Put You in Charge

Setting financial goals that are realistic and attainable can help you

- establish a basic framework for continuing financial stability
- utilize your income to the best advantage
- accept the reality of your particular financial situation, so you can learn not to spend against a dream
- examine, along with your entire family, your values and priorities
- devise ways to use your available resources to attain your goals
- take charge of your money and, even more importantly, your life.

If you and your spouse have never established goals, first think short-term. A short-term goal is something you want in the near future—say, a year or two from now. A new car? A long-deserved (and long put off?) vacation? New furniture or carpeting to replace something that's more than worn out? Whatever it is, put it on a list and give it a dollar amount and a time frame.

> **GOAL TIP:** Don't try to do it alone. Get your spouse in the act. And your kids (if they are old enough to read and write, they are old enough to listen and think and contribute, and they may even surprise you with their common sense and logic). Don't leave any member of the family out of the discussions and the decisions. Too many misunderstandings about money develop because people didn't let their goals be known and understood.

Don't be surprised to discover conflicts. You may have one supreme goal, your spouse another—and achieving one may prevent achieving the other. So recognize that desires often exceed resources, and be ready to set up priorities. Remember that if there is no real agreement on the goals, either spouse can sabotage the entire plan.

How Long Are Longer Goals?

Three to five years is a good length for a medium-term goal. This might be a major vacation trip—say, the entire family off to Europe for three or four weeks, or an addition on the house, or a daughter's wedding reception, or a new car.

> **GOAL TIP:** Yes, a new car can be a short-term or a medium-term goal. Best bet: The day you drive home a new car, make your next new car a medium-term goal, for as sure as death and taxes is the fact that an automobile (1) will wear out, (2) will cost a lot more money than today, and (3) is something you cannot do without. When you buy a new car, take out a loan for three years, pay it off and drive the car for three more years while you continue the same payments into savings. The family that disciplines itself to save so they can buy a car out

of savings (which pay interest to you), rather than by borrowing and paying out interest on the loan, is way ahead.

Long-term goals look far into the future. Ten years. Fifteen. Twenty. You name it. *Your* long-term goal is to kiss the rat race good-bye, and it is the reason why you are reading this book. For someone else, it might be the big, big house, with the in-the-ground swimming pool, the tennis court, the solarium, the quarter-acre genuine hand-made Oriental rug. Maybe for you it's both, which is fine if you can handle it.

Don't be influenced by what others do or say. Don't be put off when some of your friends are buying high-priced and high-powered cars and moving to larger homes. Let them have those goals. Only you know what you want to do with your own money. Let them think you're nuts—until you go cruising around the world or start your dreamed-of business while they are still bogged down in huge mortgages and just waking up to the need to save for retirement.

Follow Through on Established Goals

It is all well and good to establish goals, but the most important thing is to follow through. Look at your behavior. Did you meet your short-term goal? If not, why not? Was it unrealistic? Was putting away one hundred dollars a month too much? Or did it lose its importance? Did you rationalize that you didn't really want that—whatever it was—anyway? Was it something that mattered a lot to you but not so much to your spouse?

Watch out for procrastination. We are all born with a think-today brain. Tomorrow? *Mañana!* You have to fight the tendency to put off to tomorrow. To plan for tomorrow calls for beginning to act today. Right now. Organize your goals and keep a determined eye on them. When you are halfway to achieving a short-term goal, be like the determined, disciplined dieter: Allow yourself to indulge in a hot fudge sundae when you know you've gone four weeks and lost four pounds. But only one.

One more thing about goals. Realize that a short-term goal may take priority over your major long-term goal for a year or so. Some unforeseen event can impose a detour on your road map. But if your long-term goal is important, you will get back on the road and keep on toward your planned destination. With your map of goals in hand, you can recognize the detours when they appear and be ready to deal with them.

The reason for putting goals down on paper is simple and practical: It is to help you avoid waking up at the age of 55 or so to realize that, while you talked a good game, you failed to draw up a plan that was realistic and attainable.

NOTE: Inflation will have an impact on your goals. It will be important for you to take inflation into account in your saving and investing. You will want to be careful. If inflation is at 5.5 percent, for instance, and you put your money into a passbook savings account that pays 5.5 percent, that money is losing "purchasing power." The real rate of return on any savings account is the actual return the bank pays, less the rate of inflation. A medium- or long-term goal, encompassing five or more years, must include planning for inflation (see table 1).

Judy's Plans . . . Andy's Plans

At 33, Judy is thinking seriously about retiring at 45. A native of the Caribbean, she is a popular and successful real estate agent earning $60,000 a year even in the depressed real estate market of the early 1990s. Her plan is to return to her native Caribbean island, where living is inexpensive and easy. "I can't keep up this pace forever," she says. "The job is very demanding." You will see how Judy is preparing for her financial independence in chapter 18.

Andy's father died soon after retiring. He had spent 52 years as an assembly-line worker with a major Connecticut manufacturer. Andy, who is 47, said, "This won't happen to me." His plan? To retire within the next three years. How? His company provides an

Table 1. How Much Money Do You Need
to Equal $100 Today?

Years	Inflation Rate			
	3%	4%	5%	6%
5	$116	$122	$128	$134
10	134	148	163	179
15	156	180	208	240
20	181	219	265	321
25	209	267	339	429

SOURCE: *Stocks, Bonds, Bills, & Inflation 1991 Yearbook*. Ibbotson Associates, Chicago (annually updates work by Roger G. Ibbotson and Rex A. Sinquefield). All rights reserved.

excellent profit-sharing and stock-purchase plan. "We don't spend a lot of money," he says. "I drive a 1977 car and we take on no debts except our mortgage. I put everything I can into buying all the company stock they'll sell me."

Andy also has stock options, which he will exercise before he retires. Fortunately, Andy works for a highly successful company. It suffers no downturns. Andy is counting on early retirement to give him more time with his family—and to do volunteer work (he's torn between that and a new career).

More about Andy when we discuss profit-sharing.

What are *your* goals? Use worksheet I to list your short-term, mid-term, and long-term goals. Remember—don't try to do it alone. Get your spouse involved. Your goals are a joint enterprise. The amount you will need to meet your long-term goal, i.e., financial independence in 10 to 15 years, is probably hard to figure out right now. But by the time you finish this book, you should be able to fill in the long-term amount needed column.

WORKSHEET I: PERSONAL GOALS

Goal	Short-Term 0–2 years			Mid-Term 3–5 years			Long-Term 5+ years		
	Time	Amount Needed	Amount Saved	Time	Amount Needed	Amount Saved	Time	Amount Needed	Amount Saved

CHAPTER 3

Up Your Assets

Gather the Data

You cannot develop a plan for getting what you don't have until you know what you already have. "Where do we stand financially right now?" is the first question you and your spouse must ask each other if you want to enjoy financial independence in 10 to 15 years. The answers you give—the information you round up—will become the foundation for all the decisions you will then make. It must be a continually maintained foundation, updated annually or semiannually. It is, in fact, an *inventory* of your assets and liabilities.

Important: Accurate Information

You've got to begin with accurate information. I cannot stress that too strongly. You cannot make sound financial decisions for the future without gathering and maintaining personal financial information that is factual, detailed, and fully accurate. As it is in all sound money management, this financial gathering is by far the most important aspect of the task. Erroneous financial information can lead to disastrous financial decisions. It can make you think a particular financial product is right for you when it really is not. Yet the natural human tendency, to which most people succumb, is to guesstimate. Why? Because they just can't be bothered with collecting all the facts and figures they need. And then, to make matters worse, they can't be bothered with setting priorities on their spending.

Garbage In—Garbage Out

Because your plan will be only as good as the data you accumulate, your financial fact-gathering is—as it is in all sound money management—the most important aspect of the task. Incomplete information, inaccurate information, outdated information, can lead you into bad decisions.

The first time around, gathering your financial data may seem like an endless—and endlessly tedious—task. It will take time, but the resulting file will be indispensable. And it should be just that: a *file* of lists, forms, reports, statements. Once you have established this financial data file, it will be relatively quick and simple to update it once or twice a year. In fact, the smartest thing you can do is to maintain it on a month-by-month basis, keeping it in mind and near at hand as you pay bills each month.

Is the information you need hard to find, or to obtain? Some is, some isn't. Some is right at your fingertips, in bank and stockbroker statements, in your check stubs (if you are already a good record-keeper, jotting the purpose of every check on its stub), in your files (if you already maintain real files rather than a pile of stuff haphazardly thrown into a desk drawer). Some of the information, on the other hand, you will have to research and send for.

Your purpose is to gather all bits of pertinent information about your assets and liabilities, so that you can put together an accurate Net Worth Statement. It will be important, while you're at it, to develop information that is as accurate as possible about your future income and expenses.

The following list will guide you on what to round up and put together in your file. It's a good idea to use a separate file folder for each category. (Note: If some items are not readily at hand—are safer, for instance, in your safe deposit box—put a separate piece of paper in your file to identify each one.)

Handy Checklist for Taking Inventory

1. Money file
   • checking accounts: most recent bank statements
   • savings accounts: bank books or most recent statements
   • certificates of deposit
   • money-market funds
   • Treasury bills
2. Investment file
   • stocks and bonds: most recent brokerage statements
   • your own list of stocks and bonds
   • mutual funds: most recent statements
3. Pension and retirement file (most recent statements)
   • individual retirement accounts (IRAs)
   • Keogh plans
   • 401 (k) plans
   • tax-deferred annuities
   • deferred compensation plans
   • corporate pension plans
   • official company description of pension plan and policy
4. Closely-held business interests file
   • notes on current value
5. Real estate file
   • personal: home and second home—current market values
   • rental-income-producing: current income and market values
   • commercial: current and income market values
6. Life insurance file
   • policies' face values
   • current cash values
7. Other assets file
   • limited partnerships
   • oil and gas partnerships
   • collectibles (current values): gold, silver, coins, stamps, antiques, etc.

   8. Liabilities file
   - mortgages: personal
   - credit cards: American Express, VISA, MasterCard, etc.
   - charge accounts: department stores, gasoline, heating
     fuel
   - loans:
        automobile
        education
        bank (including "cash reserve" or other automatic pro-
           tection against overdraft)
        individual or personal IOUs
        brokerage margin
   - investment and/or business mortgages or loans
   9. Income and expense file
   - paycheck stub (most recent, showing year to date for all
     deductions)
   - end-of-year statements or 1099 forms showing interest
     and dividend income, from
        banks
        brokerage firms
        mutual funds
   - last three years' federal, state, and city income-tax re-
     turns
   - Social Security Statement of Benefits (see chapter 6)
   - expense worksheet (see chapter 4)
   10. Professionals/consultants file (names, addresses, phone
     numbers)
   - accountants
   - appraisers
   - brokers, business
   - brokers, real estate
   - brokers, stocks and bonds
   - financial planner
   - lawyer
   - pension expert (at employer's)

It will probably take as long as six weeks to get the information on future Social Security benefits. To get it, you will need to send Social Security a Request for Earnings and Benefit Estimate Statement, also known as Form SSA-7004-PC. You can get one at your local Social Security office, or send for it at one of the following addresses.

Social Security Administration
Albuquerque Data Operations Center
P.O. Box 4429, Station A
Albuquerque, NM 87196

Social Security Administration
Salinas Data Operations Center
100 East Alvin Drive
Salinas, CA 93906

Social Security Administration
Wilkes-Barre Data Operations Center
P.O. Box 20
Wilkes-Barre, PA 18703

Or to the following, which acts as a distribution center for the Social Security Administration:

Consumer Information Center
Dept. 74
Pueblo, CO 81009

If you're not sure if you want to retire in 10, 15, or 20 years, you'll need to send in a form for each of the projected retirement dates.

With all this information successfully gathered in its various files, and with the files in one or more file drawers or boxes, you are ready to go at the fun part: figuring out your true net worth.

This form furnished courtesy of

Request for Earnings and Benefit Estimate Statement

To receive a free statement of your earnings covered by Social Security and your estimated future benefits, all you need to do is fill out this form. Please print or type your answers. When you have completed the form, fold it and mail it to us.

1. Name shown on your Social Security card:

First   Middle Initial   Last

2. Your Social Security number as shown on your card:

☐☐☐ - ☐☐ - ☐☐☐☐

3. Your date of birth: Month   Day   Year

4. Other Social Security numbers you have used:

☐☐☐ - ☐☐ - ☐☐☐☐
☐☐☐ - ☐☐ - ☐☐☐☐

5. Your Sex: ☐ Male   ☐ Female

6. Other names you have used (including a maiden name):

7. Show your actual earnings for last year and your estimated earnings for this year. Include only wages and/or net self-employment income covered by Social Security.

A. Last year's actual earnings:

$ ☐☐☐,☐☐☐.☐☐
   Dollars only

B. This year's estimated earnings:

$ ☐☐☐,☐☐☐.☐☐
   Dollars only

8. Show the age at which you plan to retire: ☐☐
(Show only one age)

9. Below, show the average yearly amount that you think you will earn between now and when you plan to retire. Your estimate of future earnings will be added to those earnings already on our records to give you the best possible estimate.

Enter a yearly average, not your total future lifetime earnings. Only show earnings covered by Social Security. Do not add cost-of-living, performance or scheduled pay increases or bonuses. The reason for this is that we estimate retirement benefits in today's dollars, but adjust them to account for average wage growth in the national economy.

However, if you expect to earn significantly more or less in the future due to promotions, job changes, part-time work, or an absence from the work force, enter the amount in today's dollars that most closely reflects your future average yearly earnings.

Most people should enter the same amount that they are earning now (the amount shown in 7B).

Your future average yearly earnings:

$ ☐☐☐,☐☐☐.☐☐
   Dollars only

10. Address where you want us to send the statement:

Name

Street Address (Include Apt. No., P.O. Box, or Rural Route)

City   State   Zip Code

I am asking for information about my own Social Security record or the record of a person I am authorized to represent. I understand that if I deliberately request information under false pretenses I may be guilty of a federal crime and/or imprisoned. I authorize you to send the statement of earnings and benefit estimates to the person named in item 10 through a contractor.

Please sign your name (Do not print)

▲

Date   (Area Code) Daytime Telephone No.

ABOUT THE PRIVACY ACT
Social Security is allowed to collect the facts on this form under Section 205 of the Social Security Act. We need them to quickly identify your record and prepare the earnings statement you asked us for. Giving us these facts is voluntary. However, without them we may not be able to give you an earnings and benefit estimate statement. Neither the Social Security Administration nor its contractor will use the information for any other purpose.

Specifications for this form were secured from the Social Security Administration

FORM SSA-7004-PC (SPEC)(9-89) Destroy Prior Edition

We estimate that it will take you about 5 minutes to complete this form. This includes the time it will take to read the instructions, gather the necessary facts and fill out the form. If you have comments or suggestions on the estimate, or on any other aspect of this form, write to the Social Security Administration, ATTN: Reports Clearance Officer, 1-A-21 Operations Bldg., Baltimore, MD 21235, and to the Office of Management and Budget, Paperwork Reduction Project (0960-0466), Washington, D.C. 20503. Do not send completed forms or information concerning your claim to these offices.

Determine Your Net Worth

Once a Year: Your Balance Sheet

The purpose of this book is to help you understand the importance of building up your assets from now until when you retire or when you want to be financially independent. How can you tell if you really are building up your assets? You need to develop a picture of your net worth, and you should do it every year. It's what every business does. A business prepares a balance sheet at least once a year to see if it is better off than last year. It is the only way to measure progress and determine whether your assets are growing.

The income from your assets—those you have today and those you will accumulate in the future—will be your most important source of income if you plan to kiss the rat race good-bye by the time you are 45 or 50. Later on, you will be able to count on Social Security, and possibly a pension. Together, they will provide "the three-legged stool of retirement income."

Just how do you find out your net worth? First you add up all your assets—everything you own that has monetary value. Then add up your liabilities—that's everything you owe. Subtract the amount of your liabilities from the sum of your assets. The result is your net worth. (If the result is a *minus figure*—i.e., you owe more than you own—you have what is known as a *negative net worth*, and you have learned something mighty important . . . something you must start now to change to positive net worth. Living with negative net worth is living precariously; see chapter 5 on debt management.)

First the Assets

Start with the files you have gathered and organized (see "Handy Checklist for Taking Inventory" on preceding pages in this chapter). From these files, jot down all your assets on worksheet II. Note that you list, for instance, each certificate of deposit separately by ownership, so you know not only how many different CDs you have but who owns each one, how much it is worth, which bank it is at, and when it matures. Then add up all the CDs and enter the total on the Net Worth Statement.

Do the same for each item on the checklist and in your files. To find the current value of such items as stocks and bonds and mutual funds, check the financial listings in today's newspaper. For the value of real estate and personal property, remember that it is not what you "think" the property is worth, it is the price you would actually get if you put it up for sale tomorrow morning.

Two Types of Assets

Assets are of two types: those that produce income, and those that do not produce income. The income-producing ones include savings accounts, certificates of deposit, stocks, bonds, rental real estate, retirement assets (e.g., profit sharing, IRAs, etc.), the cash value of life insurance. These assets are silently working for you.

Assets that do not produce income include your home and vacation or weekend home, automobiles, home furnishings, and collectibles. It is easy to assume that these are not working for you—that, in fact, they cost you money, for you have to maintain them as part of your living expenses by paying for maintenance, utilities, taxes, and insurance. Yet some are indeed also silently working for you—particularly your home (or homes) and collectibles, which in the usual course of events are appreciating daily.

How do you know how much something is worth? Check with a couple of real estate brokers on the current value of your home. And read the real estate advertisements to find out the prices on houses similar to yours. Find out the book value of your cars and, if they are in top-notch shape, what price you could probably get by advertising in the used-car market. Clothing and home furnishings (unless they are antiques) have probably gone down in value since you bought them, but it is important to include realistic figures for them. Diamonds, rare coins, stamps, paintings, books, antiques— you can establish a reasonably accurate value for each by consulting an appraiser or, in many cases, by carefully reading the specialized magazines in their respective fields.

TIP: Be sure to use the files you compiled from the checklist to guide you on adding *hidden assets* to your numbers; these include

- Your employee benefits
- Your current vested interest in your company's pension or profit-sharing plan (i.e., how much of it you could take with you as a lump sum if you departed today; note that if only an annuity is payable upon retirement, the value to list is $0, for the annuity is a source of future income but it is not an asset)
- Current cash values of life insurance policies
- Your interest in business partnerships or other such ventures (i.e., what price you would get if you sold your interest).

List Those Liabilities

Now go back to the files and start listing your liabilities. How much is the unpaid balance on your mortgage or mortgages—on your home, vacation house, rent-producing property? What is the total balance that remains to be paid on MasterCard, VISA, department store and gasoline company accounts? How about the cash reserve in use on your checking account? Then there may be auto loans, education loans, home-improvement loans, life-insurance loans. Any taxes due on real estate or personal property? How about Federal or state taxes that are not being deducted from your paycheck? And don't forget the out-of-the-ordinary: business loans, margin-account loans, loans taken against the cash value of a life insurance policy.

Putting all these figures down on paper will prove the value of having done the job of getting your files together, for it will enable you to develop an accurate, up-to-date picture of your liabilities.

It's a good idea to double-check all your figures. Forget anything? Incomplete information now could lead to your making a

WORKSHEET II: ASSETS

Liquid Assets

Bank	Account #	Type[a]	Owner	Maturity Date	Current Value

[a]Checking, savings account, certificate of deposit, money market, savings bond, Treasury bill

Securities

Name	# Shares	Purchase Date	Purchase Price	Type[b]	Owner	Current Value

[b]Stocks, bonds, commodities, futures, options

Mutual Funds

Name	# Shares	Purchase Date	Purchase Price	Type[c]	Owner	Current Value

[c]Stock fund, bond fund, balanced fund

Real Estate

Address	Type[d]	Owner	Purchase Date	Purchase Price	Income	Mortgage Balance	Current Value

[d]Personal residence, 2nd home, income property

WORKSHEET II: ASSETS (cont.)

Retirement Assets

Type[e]	Owner	Type Investment[f]	Current Value[g]

[e]IRA, Keogh, SEP, 401(k), 403(b) annuity, pension plan, profit-sharing plan
[f]Insurance, mutual fund, certificate of deposit, stock, other
[g]For a pension plan which permits a lump-sum withdrawal, list the lump-sum amount. List a value of $0 where an annuity is payable only upon retirement—the annuity amount will be listed as a source of future income and not as an asset.

Insurance

Company	Type[h]	Face Amount	Insured	Beneficiary	Cash	Loan Amount	Cash Value

[h]Term, whole life, universal life, group life

Business Interests

Name	Address	Nature of Business	Type[i]	% of Ownership	Current Value

[i]Sole proprietorship, partnership, corporation, S corporation

Personal Property

Current Value

Home Furnishings _____

Automobiles _____

Boat _____

WORKSHEET II: ASSETS (cont.)

Jewelry/Furs _____

Collectibles _____

_____

_____

wrong decision in the future, so be sure everything that can be represented or valued in terms of dollars is included.

Now total up the assets. Then the liabilities. Subtract liabilities from assets. Now you know your net worth.

If yours is a negative net worth, don't panic. But do get serious about debt management (see chapter 5).

In addition to giving you an accurate picture of how you are building your assets for retirement, your net worth statement is an important barometer for your estate, investment, and insurance planning, as well as for debt management. You want your net worth to rise as you save and invest. If you find that your earnings are increasing but your net worth is not, you know something is wrong—your investments may have gone sour, or you have taken on too much debt. And so you must make adjustments: Assess what is going on, sell off the losing investments, reinvest, reduce your debt.

WORKSHEET III: LIABILITIES

Mortgage(s)

Bank	Acct #	Interest Rate	Property[a] Address	Borrower(s)	Balance Due

[a]Personal residence, rental property, vacation home

Installment Loan

Acct #	Type[b]	Interest Rate	Borrower	Balance Due

[b]Auto, boat, education, home improvement

Charge Accounts

Name of Store/ Bank Card	Acct #	Interest Rate	Borrower(s)	Balance Due

Other Liabilities

Type[c]	Owed to	Interest Rate	Borrower	Balance Due

[c]Margin account, life insurance, taxes due, etc.

WORKSHEET IV: NET WORTH STATEMENT

as of _____ _____, 19___

Assets

	Self	Spouse	Joint

Liquid Assets

	Self	Spouse	Joint
Cash	_____	_____	_____
Checking Accounts	_____	_____	_____
Savings Accounts	_____	_____	_____
Credit Union Accounts	_____	_____	_____
Money Market Funds	_____	_____	_____
Certificates of Deposit	_____	_____	_____
U.S. Savings Bonds	_____	_____	_____
Other	_____	_____	_____

Securities

Stocks	_____	_____	_____
Bonds, Notes	_____	_____	_____
Tax-exempt Bonds	_____	_____	_____
Mutual Funds	_____	_____	_____
Government Securities	_____	_____	_____
Other	_____	_____	_____

Other Investment Assets

Limited Partnerships	_____	_____	_____
Real Estate Rental Property	_____	_____	_____
Cash Value of Life Insurance	_____	_____	_____
Hard Assets (Precious Metals)	_____	_____	_____
Business (Stock, Ptnr'ship/ Owner)	_____	_____	_____
Trusts	_____	_____	_____
Loans to Others	_____	_____	_____
Other	_____	_____	_____

WORKSHEET IV: NET WORTH STATEMENT (cont.)

Retirement Assets

IRAs, KEOGHs, SEPs ⎯⎯ ⎯⎯ ⎯⎯

Profit Sharing, Employee
  Savings ⎯⎯ ⎯⎯ ⎯⎯

401(k), 403(b), etc. ⎯⎯ ⎯⎯ ⎯⎯

Pension (Def. Benefit/Def.
  Contrib.) ⎯⎯ ⎯⎯ ⎯⎯

Annuities (Tax Deferred/
  Single Prem.) ⎯⎯ ⎯⎯ ⎯⎯

Other ⎯⎯ ⎯⎯ ⎯⎯

Personal Assets

Homes (Personal Use) ⎯⎯ ⎯⎯ ⎯⎯

Other Real Estate ⎯⎯ ⎯⎯ ⎯⎯

Vehicles (Car, Boat, RV, etc.) ⎯⎯ ⎯⎯ ⎯⎯

Furniture & Fixtures ⎯⎯ ⎯⎯ ⎯⎯

Personal Property ⎯⎯ ⎯⎯ ⎯⎯

Collectibles ⎯⎯ ⎯⎯ ⎯⎯

Other ⎯⎯ ⎯⎯ ⎯⎯

Total Assets ══ ══ ══

Liabilities

	Self	Spouse	Joint

Short Term

Gasoline Credit Cards ⎯⎯ ⎯⎯ ⎯⎯

Store Credit Cards ⎯⎯ ⎯⎯ ⎯⎯

Major Credit Cards ⎯⎯ ⎯⎯ ⎯⎯

Vehicle Loans ⎯⎯ ⎯⎯ ⎯⎯

Taxes Due ⎯⎯ ⎯⎯ ⎯⎯

Other Personal Loans ⎯⎯ ⎯⎯ ⎯⎯

Other ⎯⎯ ⎯⎯ ⎯⎯

Total Short Term ══ ══ ══

WORKSHEET IV: NET WORTH STATEMENT (cont.)

Long Term

Home Mortgage Balances ———— ———— ————

Home Improvement Loans ———— ———— ————

Installment Loans ———— ———— ————

Education Loans ———— ———— ————

Demand Notes ———— ———— ————

Investment Loans ———— ———— ————

Leases ———— ———— ————

Life Insurance Loans ———— ———— ————

Other Long Term ———— ———— ————

Total Long Term ———— ———— ————

Total Liabilities ———— ———— ————

To figure out your net work, you must *subtract* your total liabilities from your total assets:

Total Assets ———— ———— ————

(less) Total Liabilities ———— ———— ————

Net Worth ———— ———— ————

CHAPTER 4

You Can Design Your Life-Style

"Should we eat out this often?"

"I'm not reading all these magazines—are you? Why do we subscribe to so many?"

"Can't we refinance and get this mortgage payment down lower?"

"Brown-bagging my lunch—how much will that save me?"

"A new car? Well, if we need one, let's get something less expensive."

Tough questions. They call for good hard realistic answers if you're planning on a successful early retirement. They all relate to cash flow—the money that moves in and out of your life on a daily, weekly, and monthly basis.

Understanding your cash flow is vital to understanding your total financial picture and planning your financial independence. Analyzing your cash flow is a positive step toward building a solid financial foundation. You cannot plan the most rewarding period of your life without doing a careful and thorough cash-flow analysis.

Before we get into the details of analyzing your cash flow, let's take a moment to think about your life-style. Stop and really think about it. Just what is your life-style now? And just what do you envision for those years you are planning for? Whatever it is— whether it involves entertaining and dining out (you and your spouse or the two of you and friends), being entertained (plenty of

theater, movies, video rentals, sports tickets, compact discs), cars
(recreational vehicles, antique autos, motorcycles), travel (day
trips, weekends, cruises, tours), clothes (dressy or sportswear),
active sports (golf, skiing, tennis, windsurfing, sailing or power
boating, bowling), hobbies (photography, collecting, square dancing)—or a zillion other things you do when you're not on the job
you have now, every single bit of it takes money.

How do you predict how much money you will need to continue
or expand your present life-style, or to pick up on a new one? It is
almost impossible to make such a prediction. But what you can do
is take a close look now at what your spending patterns are and
discuss—you and your spouse—how they may change if you kiss
the rat race good-bye . . . especially at the young age this book is
talking about. You can see what your spending patterns are now,
and discuss how they may change during retirement.

They will change before your target date for retirement. Your
expenses will increase. Why? Inflation.

Every Purchase Is Affected

Every purchase we make is affected by inflation. It nibbles at us
all the time, affecting especially those who are on fixed incomes.
What's the cause? Many things. Buy-now-pay-later spending, government deficits, energy demands, higher wage levels. The federal
government has a measure that reflects change in the prices we
pay for the goods and services we need or want. It's called the
Consumer Price Index (CPI). The CPI is the weighted average
of the costs of several hundred consumer items: food, clothing,
automobiles, medical services, shelter and fuel, transportation—
all the things you need for day-to-day living. It reveals the average
changes in prices, over time, of these basic consumer items, and
shows the ever-upward trend of inflation.

To cope with inflation, we have learned to work additional hours,
spend less, increase our skills as do-it-yourselfers. For many people, wages or salary increases have barely kept up with inflation,

Table 2. Inflation Factor Table

Years Before Goal Is Met	Inflation		
	3%	5%	7%
1	1.03	1.05	1.07
2	1.06	1.10	1.14
3	1.09	1.16	1.23
4	1.13	1.22	1.31
5	1.16	1.28	1.40
6	1.19	1.30	1.50
7	1.23	1.41	1.61
8	1.27	1.48	1.72
9	1.30	1.55	1.84
10	1.34	1.63	1.97
11	1.38	1.71	2.10
12	1.43	1.80	2.25
13	1.47	1.89	2.40
14	1.51	1.98	2.58
15	1.56	2.08	2.76

if that. Those whose incomes have grown faster than inflation have been lucky, for they could either save more or spend more.

Think of inflation as a fixed expense. How much should you fix it at? Take the number of years between now and the retirement you're planning: say, 15 years, for example. If a 5 percent rate of inflation continues for 15 years, the inflation factor will be 2.08. That means that something that costs $5,000 today will cost a little more than $10,000 in 15 years.

Expenses Will Change

When you retire, your expenses will change. Commutation, gasoline, tolls, lunches out, clothing, take-out dinners—all those costs will go down or disappear. You will no longer have to pay into Social Security (unless you continue to have earned income). Probably your income taxes will go down. And you will have no payroll deductions for savings plans. But some things will go up: hobbies, travel, medical (insurance, unreimbursed medical and dental bills, and drugs), food consumed at home. Even your utilities cost can rise, if you have both been out of the house during working hours and the thermostat has been turned back for nine or ten hours of the working day. And it is highly likely that your entertainment costs will rise.

Also, don't forget that if you are setting up a new business, you will have at least minimal expenses for a telephone answering machine, plus FAX, computer, maybe a copier and other items.

Where Does It Come From? Where Does It Go? Cash Flow

The best tool available to help you know where your money not only comes from but where it goes is your own cash flow statement. It tracks your income and expenses over a period of time, and tells you what your spending patterns are. It can help prevent impulse spending and guide you in deciding what you can and cannot afford as well as in increasing saving for specific financial goals.

Your cash flow statement organizes your spending by categories. Probably you know, off-hand, what you spend on electricity and food and, for instance, automobile insurance. But few people ever add up all their spending in all categories and give themselves an accurate picture of their total spending for the year.

Income and Deductions

Take a look at worksheet V, the cash flow statement. On it, list your present sources of income: salary or salaries, interest, dividends. Are you divorced? Don't forget alimony and child support.

If you work on commission, as a real estate agent, stockbroker, or salesperson—or if you're a farmer—be conservative. Estimate your income from last year's, or make an educated guess for the next couple of months. Watch your actual income, compared to your estimate, over at least that long, so you see where your peaks and valleys are.

If you work in a seasonal business, of course, you already know that in certain months your income is higher than in others. The important thing is that you take into consideration the fact that your situation is different from those who receive a fixed paycheck every month.

Now make some deductions. From your gross income, take away the amount your employer deducts for Social Security, Federal and state taxes, company benefits that you pay for (e.g., major medical insurance, life insurance), and savings such as 401(k) plan. You may prefer to list the savings under the fixed-expenses heading. That is good self-psychology, for any money that can be deducted as savings is money that is not available for spending.

Fixed Expenses

Under Fixed Expenses, list all those things you pay the same for—or just about the same—every month: your mortgage or rent, condo fees, utilities, commutation, and installment credit payments. Now take those expenses that you pay quarterly, semiannually, or annually, such as real estate and personal property taxes, insurance premiums, club dues. Good idea: On this list, include the amount you have deducted from your paycheck for savings (401(k) plan, payroll savings plan, etc.), an amount for regular personal saving, and a set amount that you will earmark as your emergency fund.

What is an emergency fund? It is money you set aside for emergencies that are too big to be included in everyday expenses, and that are not covered by insurance. It is for those unexpected expenses that always turn up just as you thought everything was on an even keel: the big repair bill on the car, the new tires, the medical emergency that is not fully covered by insurance, the fender bender that costs only as much as your deductible, the stretch of unemployment you never expected to happen, the collapse of the washing machine that you thought would keep working forever, the airline tickets when a serious illness or sudden death in the family—or, more happily, the wedding of a niece or nephew or cousin—calls you across the country.

Your emergency fund is a cushion. It lets you avoid putting such sudden costs on a credit card or, even worse, taking out a personal loan. How much should you put into it? At least three to six months' net income. If you are young, both working, and have a new car and new appliances, three months' income is a safe bet. But as you get toward your retirement date, you will need to keep a six-month cushion for emergencies. Then, once you have set aside enough money in this fund, you can start saving for something else. The important point: Get money into that emergency fund before you think of anything else.

Total and divide by 12 to get the average monthly amount of your fixed expenses. Some months it will actually be higher, some months lower, but you must have this much in your fixed expenses account each month. You can maintain it in a separate interest-bearing account. Keep this account separate from other accounts, and use it only to pay the fixed expenses items as they come due each month or quarter or year.

Flexible Expenses

As the name implies, these are the expenses that can vary from month to month: food, clothing, transportation, gifts, entertainment, household maintenance, laundry and dry cleaning, purchases for the household. Let the worksheet help you categorize them. It will probably remind you of some you don't think about, but that add up each month.

TIP: Include among flexible expenses "mad money" every month. Everyone needs to feel that there is some money that does not have to be accounted for.

Here's hoping you have some good records of your spending over at least the past year or so. Review those figures. They will be invaluable. If you don't have records, *start today* to keep a record of *all* your spending over the next 6 to 12 months. You will build an accurate picture of what your spending patterns are.

If you have a personal computer (PC), check out the various software programs for handling money. Many inexpensive programs are available that track your expenses. Each has an abundance of categories. You can easily delete those you don't need (e.g., no pets at your house? don't use the "Pets" category) and add any that are uniquely yours (e.g., VCR rentals, as distinguished from entertainment in general, or skiing rather than general recreation). This invaluable tool can make your life a lot easier.

How to Watch the Cash Move

You have only three choices about how to pay for things: with cash, by check, or on credit.

Cash is dangerous stuff. It is hard to categorize. You get cash from the Automatic Teller Machine (ATM). Or you make a check out to cash. Before you know it, the cash is gone (leaked through your fingers, as they say?) and you cannot account for it. Too often, withdrawals from the ATM don't even get entered in the checkbook. That delivers a rude awakening when the bank statement comes along at the end of a month—or, even sooner, a notice that you are overdrawn arrives in the morning mail.

Best idea, if you must use cash, is to carry a pocket notebook and jot down your cash expenditures—yes, make yourself do this!—as they occur. After a few weeks or a couple of months, you will recognize the categories of spending that you are using cash for. Once a month, or at least once a quarter, enter all these figures in

WORKSHEET V: CASH FLOW STATEMENT

Income

	Wife	Husband	Joint
Earned Income			
Salary/Wages	————	————	————
Bonus	————	————	————
Commissions	————	————	————
Investment Income			
Interest	————	————	————
Dividends	————	————	————
Capital Gains	————	————	————
Rental Income	————	————	————
Other			
Alimony/Child Support	————	————	————
Trust Income	————	————	————
Gifts	————	————	————
Other	————	————	————

Deductions

	Wife	Husband	Joint
Social Security	————	————	————
Federal Income Tax	————	————	————
State Income Tax	————	————	————
Work-Related Benefits[a]	————	————	————
Medical Insurance	————	————	————
Life Insurance	————	————	————
Other	————	————	————

[a]Deductions for savings plans are under Savings or Set-asides (see p. 41).

your cash flow statement. Round them up or down to the nearest dollar (big figures to the nearest $10).

Paying by check is better. The grocery store, the dry cleaner, the card shop, the beauty parlor—they will all take checks. If they don't know you, usually you need only show your driver's license (sometimes a major credit card, too) and they will accept your check. This may take a couple of minutes, but it does provide an accurate record of your expense. Just be sure to fill in your checkbook stub with a note on *exactly* what the purchase was.

> **TIP:**   One of the best habits you'll ever form is this: *Before* you write any check, whether at your desk at home or leaning on the counter in a store, write the stub—no matter how much of a hurry you are in. If a million people had this habit, a million oh-my-goshes and searchings of memory would be avoided.

The third way to pay is by credit card. Be sure to collect all receipts for credit card purchases. Put them on a spindle or in an envelope and, at the end of every month, categorize the actual purchases. Be sure not to confuse this with whatever total amount you are paying off in installments on your credit card statement. What you want, for your cash-flow picture, is an accurate record of all purchases.

TIPS:
- Don't nickel and dime it. Round up or down to the nearest dollar, big figures to $10. Otherwise, you'll go crazy.
- Decide who will pay the bills and who will do the record keeping. Work this out with other members of the family, so it is well understood and agreed upon.
- Keep it simple. Report the essentials. Don't get bogged down in too much detail, or overdo the paperwork.

Now total it all up. Any surprises? If your goal is early retirement and you find that your expenses are almost equal to—or more than—your income, it is time to take a close look and figure out just where you can cut down. If saving is a priority, and you discover that you are not saving, it is time to stop that leak and reallocate. By carefully controlling your expenditures, you can actually increase the amount of money you have available to save and invest for the ultimate promotion you want to give yourself.

	Jan	Feb	Mar	Apr	May	Jun	Jul	Aug	Sep	Oct	Nov	Dec	Total
SAVINGS OR SET-ASIDES													
At Work (401(k), etc.)													
Wife													
Husband													
Emergency Fund													
Goals													
Savings/Investment													
Other													
TOTAL SAVINGS													
FIXED EXPENSES													
Mortgage/Rent													
Condo Common Charges													
Utilities													
Electricity													
Oil/Gas													
Telephone													
Water													
Insurance													
Life													
Disability													
Auto													
Homeowner's													
Liability													
Medical													
Taxes													
Real Estate													
Estimated Fed.													
Estimated State													
Personal Property													
Debt													
Auto Loan #1													
Auto Loan #2													
Education Loan													
Credit Card #1													
Credit Card #2													
Credit Card #3													
Other Debt													
Alimony/Child Support													

FLEXIBLE EXPENSES	Jan	Feb	Mar	Apr	May	Jun	Jul	Aug	Sep	Oct	Nov	Dec	Total
Food													
Groceries													
Lunches at Work													
Household Supplies													
Meals Brought In													
Liquor/Wine													
Cigarettes													
Clothing													
Husband													
Wife													
Children													
Shoes/Shoe Repairs													
Dry Cleaning/Laundry													
Alterations													
Personal Care													
Beauty Salon—Wife													
Barber—Husband													
Haircuts—Children													
Cosmetics													
Other													
Home Maintenance													
Lawn/Garden/Trees													
Snow Plowing													
General Upkeep/Repairs													
Cleaning													
Garbage													
Exterminator													
Improvements/Major Repairs													
Miscellaneous Purchases													
(linens, small appliances,													
pots & pans)													
Furnishings/Redecorating													
Transportation													
Gas/Oil													
Routine Maintenance													
Major Repairs													
Commutation													
Taxi/Bus/Subway													
Parking/Tolls													
Driver's Licenses													
Car Registration													
Pet Expenses													
Veterinarian													
Food													
Grooming/Boarding													

	Jan	Feb	Mar	Apr	May	Jun	Jul	Aug	Sep	Oct	Nov	Dec	Total
Publications													
Books													
Magazines													
Newspapers													
Children's Expenses													
Allowance													
Baby Sitters													
Child Care													
Lessons													
Camp/Recreation													
Entertainment													
Dinners Out													
Movies/Theater													
Sporting Events													
Cable TV/													
Video Rentals													
Recreation													
Club Dues/Fees													
Equipment													
Hobbies													
Gifts/Cards													
Birthdays													
Christmas													
Graduations													
Weddings/Showers													
Miscellaneous													
Vacation(s)													
Education													
Tuition													
Room/Board													
Books/Supplies													
Travel													
Charitable Contributions													
Church/Synagogue													
Other													
Home Office & Misc.													
Stamps/Stationery													
Film/Developing													
Computer Supplies													
Medical (Unreimbursed)													
Doctor													
Dentist													
Physical Therapist													
Medicines/Drugs													
TOTAL FLEXIBLE EXPENSES													
TOTAL EXPENSES													

Now Think Budget

Chances are you will need to make some decisions on cutting down in some areas in order to have more money in others. Even if such decisions are not called for, setting up and maintaining a budget is a good idea (if you don't already have that habit).

Think of a budget as a blueprint for a building, or as a road map. It is a working tool. It need not be rigid or complicated. It will help you meet your goal of saving—saving more by cutting back in one category or another.

Your cash flow statement is the key to your budget. Now that you have worked it up, you can see where you are currently spending your money. Study it. Do you want to keep that spending plan, that road map, just the way it is? Where should you change it? What are your top priorities? What would you rather do in this category or that?

This is where the life-style questions come in. Now it is time to think about needs versus wants. You "want" to retire early. What you "need" to spend between now and that moment is up to you. How much to cut back here, how much to reallocate to there (i.e., to saving and investing) is up to you.

Now you need a notebook—something in which to list your own particular categories. Write in what you plan to spend each month, based on your past spending patterns as revealed in your cash flow statement and your analysis of those numbers as they relate to your life-style. At the end of the month, put down the amount you actually spent. That is what you then list on your next cash flow statement. (See Worksheet VI to see how to set this up.)

Remember the suggestion on page 38 about using a personal computer. Suppose you have budgeted four hundred dollars a month for groceries. In June you spend five hundred dollars. The computer will not yell and scream at you for going over budget that month. But the computer will tell you if your year-to-date total or your monthly average is on target. In many categories, such as gifts and clothing, you are not spending the same amount each month, so it's important to watch the year-to-date totals.

WORKSHEET VI: BUDGET

	Month 1 Name of Month			Month 2 Name of Month		
	Amount Estimated	Amount Spent	Difference	Amount Estimated	Amount Spent	Difference
Food						
Groceries						
Lunches at Work						
Household Supplies						
Meals Brought In						
Liquor/Wine						
Cigarettes						
Clothing						
Husband						
Wife						
Children						
Shoes/Shoe Repairs						
Dry Cleaning/Laundry						
Alterations						
Personal Care						
Beauty Salon—Wife						
Barber—Husband						
Haircuts—Children						
Cosmetics						
Other						
Home Maintenance						
Lawn/Garden/Trees						
Snow Plowing						
General Upkeep/Repairs						
Cleaning						
Garbage						
Exterminator						
Improvements/Major Repairs						
Miscellaneous Purchases						
(linens, small appliances,						
pots & pans)						
Furnishings/Redecorating						
Transportation						
Gas/Oil						
Routine Maintenance						
Major Repairs						
Commutation						

WORKSHEET VI: BUDGET (cont.)

	Month 1 Name of Month			Month 2 Name of Month		
	Amount Estimated	Amount Spent	Difference	Amount Estimated	Amount Spent	Difference
Taxi/Bus/Subway						
Parking/Tolls						
Driver's Licenses						
Car Registration						
Pet Expenses						
Veterinarian						
Food						
Grooming/Boarding						
Publications						
Books						
Magazines						
Newspapers						

Keep It Flexible . . . Include the Family

You need more than accurate records. You need family cooperation to get them and maintain them. Everyone in the family must be willing to make keeping track of household expenses a success. Consult one and all, including older children. If they are old enough to be learning arithmetic and money values in school, they are old enough to participate in family financial tracking. Certainly any child who is on an allowance should be consulted and included regularly.

Important: Remember that the wants and needs of each member of the family must be taken into consideration. An arbitrary cut in spending by one member of the family, made without consulting others, can lead to sabotage of the entire plan.

Flexibility is important, too. Emergencies will come up, plans will change, priorities will shift. You cannot set your budget in concrete. But if you know where you are now and where you want to go, you can make changes to cope with various contingencies.

Remember that a road map usually shows you more than one way to get from here to there.

Don't get so focused on early retirement that you forget to take care of your wants as well as your needs. If your plan is so inflexible that it gives you no breathing room, it is likely to self-destruct. So recognize the difference between self-denial and self-restraint. Suppose you are going to celebrate a major wedding anniversary. Not to go to the absolutely most expensive restaurant in town is self-restraint. But to go to McDonald's is self-denial.

In other words, know when to compromise. Communicate with your spouse, with your children. Recognize that there are pros and cons for spending one way or another, and that family sanity must be kept. All hands must feel that they are in a win/win situation.

Check It Out Once a Year

Be sure to review this guide, this road map, once a year. Any budget needs adjusting at least that often. Ask yourselves if your goals are being met. Are there new priorities? New goals to be set? Use your cash flow statement and your budget as tools to take you, via detours if necessary, to your destination.

A DOZEN MONEY-SAVING TIPS:

• Watch the impulse buying. Have a shopping list in hand when you walk into a store, and stick to it. Retailers, especially grocery stores, know that people spend big—as high as 40 percent of their total purchases—on things they never intended to buy when they left home. Why do you think the magazines, chewing gum, candy, etc., are hanging on the racks where you stand in line at the checkout?

• Pace your spending. If impulse says, "Get this now," take a hike out around the mall or stop for a cup of coffee and think it over. It may not seem so important 10 minutes from now, or tomorrow morning.

• Double-check the price on any major purchase. It will be worth taking the time to see what the same item costs in another store, or made by another brand. Comparison shopping can be well worth the time and effort. Check consumer publications for quality, durability, and operating costs.

• Take advantage of seasonal buys. There really are bargains in January and February, when people are paying Christmas bills and merchants must offer real come-ons to get them back into the stores. Car dealers do still introduce the new models early in the fall—and offer good buys on this year's stock that is still on hand. Air conditioners, electric fans and heaters, seasonal sportswear— you can save money on these and many other items by buying them at the right time.

• Be consistent in your saving. Set a certain amount to be saved every month—always the same exact amount—rather than trying to put aside a big amount once or twice a year. With compound interest, your money will be growing faster, day in, day out.

• Beware the sale. Before you know it, a bargain gets expensive—when the perfect skirt needs shoes to match, or the new shirt calls for a spectacular new necktie.

• Go in with neighbors on a snowblower or a leafblower. Take turns using it (but make sure someone sees to the upkeep). You can save real money on an item you don't use every day.

• But don't go into a store with a friend when you're "just shopping." No matter how strong you think your willpower is, the power of suggestion from your pal may be stronger. And then you spend money you never intended to spend.

• Clip money-saving coupons from newspapers, magazines, supplements in your Sunday paper—*and use them before they expire*. But only when they're for items you will really buy.

• Discipline yourselves to have the drinks and hors d'oeuvres at home before you go out to dinner with friends. And find the good food that's served where you don't have to pay for the flashy atmosphere. Also, watch the extras—very few of us need the whole soup-to-nuts dinner these days.

• Check out the consignment shops. You can find excellent buys on clothing—especially women's and children's.

• Make gifts—with the kids. Christmas is merrier and less costly when creative minds and hands put gifts together.

And the list goes on. Think about it. You can come up with another dozen in the next five minutes.

How Three People Look at Cash Flow

Judy's cash flow is unusual. She takes savings right off the top, carefully making sure her retirement comes first in her life. "I'm too busy to socialize," she says, "but I do allow for expensive vacations. That's when I splurge and recharge my batteries."

Ken and Shelley's combined income before retirement was more than $80,000 a year. During the year just before he retired, they made it a point to live entirely on his income—about $45,000— which was slightly less than the retirement income they expected. They changed some of their life-style habits, giving up costly lunches when they were on the road and using their camper rather than motels when they made overnight trips to crafts fairs.

Dee's house helps keep her cash flow moving. The apartment upstairs brings in $1,300 a month, and a roomer downstairs (who has kitchen privileges) pays $500 a month. Dee pays $1,200 a month on her mortgage, so she is $600 ahead every month. As an airline stewardess, she is out of the house a third of the time, so she doesn't mind having the tenants and sharing the kitchen. Considering the cutbacks her airline has imposed, the $600 is an integral part of her income. "The house had to work for me," she says. "And so far, it really does."

If both you and your spouse are working, consider saving everything that one of you brings home. This may be tough to do at first, but try it. Start with saving, let's say, a third or half of that salary and increase it every year.

CHAPTER 5

Managing Your Debt

"Buy now, pay later."

We all know what that means. But we don't like to think about it. We have developed the convenient inflationary habit of living on borrowed funds, believing that we will pay our bills tomorrow with cheaper dollars. But lately we have begun to realize that today's paycheck does not take care of yesterday's excess spending.

When the Diner's Club was started in 1950, the total outstanding consumer debt (excluding home mortgages) of the American consumer stood at $21.5 billion. Forty years later, the figure had reached $750 billion—a figure far more vast than the growth of the population could have caused. We have spent and spent, toting up debt after debt. One after another, millions of us have stretched our paychecks to and beyond the breaking point, going in over our heads in debt to support our elevated standard of living.

This is probably the highest hurdle you must face if you are serious about stepping out of the rat race. It is essential that you keep your credit obligations under control—indeed, to a minimum—during your working years. Debt has a greater likelihood than any other element of sabotaging your plans. Compulsive spending, or even well-considered spending that involves heavy debt, must not be part of your life-style.

What? No Credit Cards?

Does this mean you must not use credit cards? No. Credit cards are a great convenience. They are useful when you are traveling. They are lifesavers in an emergency. They make shopping at home from catalogs, using 800 phone numbers and no stamps or envelopes, easy as pie. They give you a "free ride" for 45 to 55 days (i.e., you pay no interest charges or fees) if you pay your balance in full each month. (But don't take cash advances—they give you no free ride; you pay interest from day one.)

Credit card financing is highly expensive when you spread payments over time, for you are renting money at a price—the interest rate. And your credit card obligations must be paid every month, just like your rent or mortgage payments. Some things that most of us know, but don't think about when we should, about credit cards:

- When interest rates rise, you pay the lender more for the money you borrow.
- The creditor takes the finance charge from your payment before deducting anything from the balance you owe.
- If you pay only the minimum amount requested, your finance charges compound.
- Since the minimum payment requested is mostly interest (or finance charge), the principal amount you owe will be reduced very, very slowly.
- The interest charged on credit cards by lending institutions (i.e., banks) is usually at a much higher rate than other types of credit (i.e., consumer loans).

Since your goal is to free up as much money as possible for saving and investing toward your retirement, now is the time to take a good hard look at how you are handling credit and debt. Are you robbing Peter to pay Paul? Borrowing to meet daily expenses or to buy the groceries? Lengthening the time between payments? Charging on credit cards the ordinary items that have life spans shorter than the time it will take to pay for them? Taking cash advances so you can buy the things you used to pay cash for? Any of these—and certainly all of them—are signs of trouble.

Start Kicking the Debt Habit

Begin by making an accurate list of all your current debt obligations, showing how much you are paying each month as well as the total amount of your debt (the latter should by now be listed in your net worth statement as a liability). Leave one item *off* this list of monthly debt payments: your home mortgage. But note that your mortgage, property taxes, and homeowner's insurance should not be higher than 25 to 30 percent of your gross pay.

Now find out what your debt ratio is. It is the percentage of your take-home pay (i.e., your gross income minus all deductions) that is needed each month to repay debt. What is a safe ratio? Credit counselors suggest that the maximum amount of a family's take-home pay that can safely go for debt payment is 15 percent. If it rises above 20 percent, most people find that they are in trouble.

When you pay off a loan, your debt ratio will change. But beware. Many people fall into the trap of taking on a bigger loan obligation as soon as they have successfully paid one off. This puts you into a higher and more dangerous debt situation.

The more you keep debt within your means, holding down those interest payments, the more income you can put into saving and investing. In fact, if you make the wise decision to cut back, you may have to spend a year or so concentrating on repaying your current debts and, simultaneously, *not* adding new ones. Tough to do. But you can do it. How? By being Draconian: by cutting your credit cards in half with a strong pair of scissors, or by turning them over to a friend who puts them in his or her safe deposit box for a year, by cutting down on all living expenses that are not absolutely necessary, by guarding against impulse spending to "lift my spirits," by paying cash and cash only at every cash register.

TIP: A good question to ask yourself about every purchase you are about to charge is this: Would I buy this if I were paying cash? When the answer is no, you begin to see that deferred spending is often avoided spending. And avoided spending can turn into savings. *Remember: Your goal is not only to reduce debt but to free up money that can be saved for retirement.*

Some Wise Ways with Credit

• Save on annual fees by eliminating some of your cards. And watch the cards that advertise that they are "free." Usually that is a promotional gimmick, lasting only through the first year, to get you signed up.

• Check the annual percentage rates (APR). This is the cost of buying an item or service on time, expressed as a percentage of your unpaid balance. Obviously, you want a card with the lowest APR. But remember, the bank can increase the interest as often and as high as it wants, up to the limit set by your state's usury laws. Such laws vary from state to state, so you should check on the limits on your present cards.

• Good credit-handling method: Maintain two cards. Put all your large purchases (e.g., a new suit or coat, compact disc player, luggage, travel) on one card, knowing you are going to pay this one over time. Put small items (e.g., a shirt or blouse, compact disc, cosmetics) on a separate card—*and pay it off in full each month.* No need to pay a finance charge on small purchases. Working this way—*thinking* this way—does not come easily. You have to start in and do it, then keep at it. It will make no sense if you lapse into letting your "small purchases" credit card slide into paying interest charges, especially now that such charges are no longer tax deductible.

• Watch out for cards that impose a finance charge each time you make a purchase, even though you are paying the bill in full each month. Most cards give you a grace period—usually 25 to 30 days from the end of the billing cycle until your payment is due. Take advantage of this "free ride." Check the date, shown on your statement, when your billing cycle begins. If you make a purchase immediately after that date, you gain free credit for 45 to 60 days. Here's how it works:

> Suppose your billing date is July 1. If you buy something on July 2, that purchase will not appear on your bill until August's statement. You will then have until the end of August to pay the bill before you incur a finance charge. But be careful: Banks do not allow the grace period if you have any unpaid balance from the previous month. Check your bank's terms.

• Always pay your credit obligations on time. Otherwise, you will be paying a delinquency penalty—a late charge—in addition to paying interest. And late payments show up on your credit rating.

• It all boils down to this: If you can't afford to pay cash, you can't afford to buy it on credit. A finance charge is money spent for nothing more than convenience.

What about Home Equity Loans?

Thanks mainly to the tax laws and the skyrocketing values of homes during the 1980s, the home equity loan has become extremely popular. Tax reform phased out deductions for interest paid for consumer credit and cash-reserve-in-use on checking accounts, but continued to permit deductions for interest paid on home mortgages, including home equity loans.

When you take out a home equity loan, you are borrowing against the value of your house. The bank looks at the market value of your home, takes a percentage of that value, deducts outstanding mortgages or liens against the property, and approves a loan for the difference. In other words, you are borrowing some of the money that you would have if you sold your home and paid off all existing liens.

Many home equity loans are set up like a revolving line of credit, giving you access to the line at any time. The bank gives you a checkbook, and you write checks up to the maximum of your credit line. You pay interest only on the amount you actually use. On most home equity loans, the interest rate is variable and moves up or down depending on the current market rate—the rate will vary from half a point to two points above prime.

Once your loan has been approved, you can use the funds for anything—major home improvements, children's education, travel, consolidating consumer debt (and thus avoiding paying interest that is not tax deductible and is probably at a much higher rate than your home equity loan), starting or expanding a business. BUT BE CAREFUL—Always keep in mind that the home equity loan was designed to finance major investments, not daily living expenses.

In fact, caution is the word if you are getting a home equity loan. You are borrowing against one of your most valuable assets—your home. If you fail to make the monthly payments, you can lose the roof over your head. So don't take on more of this kind of debt than you can handle.

How much can you safely borrow? The lender will make a well-informed decision on that, based on the current equity you have in your home and on your ability to repay the loan. They will take a good hard look at your credit history, your income, and your other current debt obligations. The upper limit on most home equity loans is 70 to 80 percent of the house's current appraised value, minus the balance yet to be paid on the existing mortgage. Or the limit may be lower, depending on the lender's conclusions about your ability to repay.

TIP: Pay close attention to how your home equity loan is to be repaid. Some lenders offer "interest only" monthly payments. When you pay interest only, you gain a nice tax deduction but you are in a risky situation, for you are not repaying any principal. That means the principal will be due as one lump sum at the end of the term of the loan. Other lenders offer "interest only" for the first 10 years but you then repay principal along with the interest for the rest of the term. So it pays to shop around. In fact, it pays to shop around for *any* type of loan—automobile, home improvement, home equity, whatever.

When you're getting ready to kiss the rat race good-bye, a home equity credit line is something to think about *because* the lender is taking a close look at your income. It will be a lot easier to get the credit line while you are still employed, and that credit line could come in handy if you're starting up a business. But *think twice about it*. After you retire, will you still be able to handle the monthly obligation? And if you think you might be using the funds for general living expenses, forget it.

The bottom line to remember is that the interest you pay on the credit you use is money gone. It can rob you of funds you need to save and invest. Careful debt management can make the difference between launching yourself into independence when you want it or working to pay off debt obligations until you are 65 years old. So now is the time to reevaluate your current credit needs and how you plan to handle them in the future. You might just want to change the way you use credit.

How Ellen and Michael Kept Debt Down

Like many couples who have kissed the rat race good-bye, Ellen and Michael were college professors who stayed in what many people would have considered a starter home. They watched their neighbors move in and move out as they took on more expensive homes and larger mortgages. "We had our hearts set on being able to retire by the time we were 45, so we decided to stay put and pay off our smaller mortgage as soon as we could," says Michael. "We didn't suffer. We maintained the house and added a bathroom and a porch and upgraded the kitchen. But what we did was always affordable in relation to our total plan."

Ellen adds, "And today—well, we see some of our old neighbors having a real struggle keeping up with the mortgage payments they've signed up for. And that's not to mention the fancy imported cars they're paying off. We've always bought good used cars and been perfectly happy."

Today Ellen and Michael are busier and happier than ever, working in second careers. Michael, who taught economics, is now deep into natural resources as a consultant to environmentalists. (His area of expertise is western water.) Ellen is in the same field, which she taught, also as a consultant. Between consulting assignments, they backpack in Alaska, trek in Nepal, and snorkel in the Bahamas.

CHAPTER 6

Social Security

No matter how old or young you are when you retire, sooner or later you are going to find yourself sitting on a stool that has three legs. One leg is Social Security. Another is your company pension. The third is your own assets: your savings and investments. Let's take a good look at each, beginning with Social Security.

Social Security will not kick in until you reach 62, which is certainly many years after you kiss the rat race good-bye. But since you have been contributing since you started work, and will continue to contribute as you move into another career (assuming you have earned income), it is important for you to understand the Social Security system and what you will ultimately receive in benefits.

The same applies to a pension. You may receive a pension when you step off the full-time treadmill, or your benefits may be frozen until you reach what your company defines as "early retirement age"—age 55 at most companies. Pensions will be discussed at length in the next chapter.

Just What Is Social Security?

The original idea when Congress passed the Social Security Act in 1933 was for the federal government to provide old-age insurance. Monthly payments to individuals who had reached the age of 65 began in 1940. Over the years, coverage has been widened, qualifications have been liberalized, and benefits have been added and increased.

In its first 40 years, the system was pretty much pay-as-you-go. In other words, almost all the money that went into the system was paid out in benefits. Then, in 1983, the Social Security Administration began looking ahead. In order to build up reserves, it increased the taxes (formerly called "contributions") coming into the system, so that today the government collects more than $110 million more—every day—than it pays out to beneficiaries. This surplus will rise until about the year 2030.

Currently, about three workers pay for each retiree. By 2020, two workers will support one retiree. And by 2035, according to today's estimates, the anticipated revenues will not be enough to pay for the obligations of the program. Obviously, Social Security will have to change in the future to cope with its increased obligations. If you were born during the baby-boom years between 1945 and 1964 (or, in fact, *any* time since 1945), any changes will affect you.

Some changes have already been made. One is to raise the retirement age from 65 to 67. Beginning in the year 2000, a gradual rise will occur. By 2022, you will have to be 67 to be eligible to start full benefits. This change will help keep the Social Security Trust solvent as well as take into account anticipated increases in life expectancy. Anyone born after 1937 will be affected (i.e., anyone who is 62 in the year 2000).

How Does It Work?

You start building up protection the first time any employer withholds Social Security taxes from your pay. But you do not start with full protection. You achieve this status by earning what Social Security calls "quarters of coverage." It takes 40 quarters of coverage for you to become fully insured—entitled to all the benefits that Social Security provides. Forty quarters is 10 years. The quarters do not have to be consecutive.

The more you earn during working years, the more Social Secu-

Table 3. Earnings Subject to Social Security Tax

1970	$ 7,800	1982	$32,400
1971	7,800	1983	35,700
1972	9,000	1984	37,500
1973	10,800	1985	39,600
1974	13,200	1986	42,000
1975	14,100	1987	43,800
1976	15,300	1988	45,000
1977	16,500	1989	48,000
1978	17,700	1990	51,300
1979	22,900	1991	53,400
1980	25,900	1992	55,500
1981	29,700		

rity will pay you when you are eligible for retirement benefits. The maximum for someone retiring at 65 in, say, 1992 is about $13,000 a year.

It is not only your own money, withheld from your pay, that goes into the Social Security Trust Fund. Your employer is required by law to put in an equal amount. (If you are self-employed, you must pay in twice as much as you would if you were on a company payroll, for no matching contribution is going in.)

What determines how much is taken out of your pay? A certain percentage of your pay is withheld each payday until your annual earnings have reached a certain amount. In 1992, the rate is 7.65 percent, and it is withheld until you have earned $55,500. If you earn between $55,500 and $130,200, Social Security gets another 1.45 percent of your pay and puts it toward the cost of Medicare. Historically, the maximum earnings amount has risen substantially since 1970, when it was $7,800. (See table 3.)

Who Gets How Much?

How much you get depends on when you start to collect benefits and on the amount you earned that was subject to Social Security tax. You can start to collect any time after you reach age 62. The later you start, up to age 70, the more you get. (More about that on subsequent pages.)

Your spouse is also entitled to benefits, even if he or she has never worked, at age 62. If your spouse has not worked, he or she is entitled to 37.5 percent of the amount of your benefit if the spouse starts to collect it at age 62. If the spouse waits until 65, the benefit increases to 50 percent as much as yours.

Suppose your spouse *has* been employed, but according to the tables his or her earnings records indicate benefits that are less than 50 percent as much as yours. He or she will nevertheless get the full 50 percent (if you are 65) or 37.5 percent (if you are 62).

If, on the other hand, your spouse has worked enough to be entitled—on his or her own—to a benefit that is greater than 50 percent as much as yours, he or she can collect on his or her own record. In other words, each who has worked for an employer outside the home can collect benefits based upon his or her own individual earnings and years of service.

A fully disabled worker, a surviving spouse who is 60 or older or who is caring for a child under 16, and a deceased worker's child who is under age 18 (or 19, if a full-time high-school student)—all may also receive Social Security benefits.

When You Quit Affects How Much You Get

You can start collecting your Social Security benefits when you turn 62. But you will pay a penalty for the privilege, for you will receive 20 percent less than if you wait until you are 65. The money you receive during those three years will put you ahead by about 12 years. That is, someone who waits until age 65 to start collecting benefits will need to collect them for 12 years to catch up with someone who starts collecting benefits at 62.

Puzzling? Look at it this way: If you receive $800 a month at age 62 rather than waiting to receive $1,000 a month at 65, you will have given up $200 a month in order to get your benefits early. During those three years, your total will come to $28,800 (36 pay-

Table 4. Benefit Reductions, Month by Month

Multiply your estimated benefit at age 65 by the reduction factor for the month in which you plan to retire and you'll see approximately how much you'll receive. Table 1 is for people who qualify for benefits through their own work records; table 2 is for spousal benefits.

Table 1				Table 2			
Months before 65	Reduction Factor	Months before 65	Reduction Factor	Months before 65	Reduction Factor	Months before 65	Reduction Factor
1	.994	19	.894	1	.993	19	.868
2	.989	20	.889	2	.986	20	.861
3	.983	21	.883	3	.979	21	.854
4	.978	22	.878	4	.972	22	.847
5	.972	23	.872	5	.965	23	.840
6	.967	24	.867	6	.958	24	.833
7	.961	25	.861	7	.951	25	.826
8	.956	26	.856	8	.944	26	.819
9	.950	27	.850	9	.938	27	.813
10	.944	28	.844	10	.931	28	.806
11	.939	29	.839	11	.924	29	.799
12	.933	30	.833	12	.917	30	.792
13	.928	31	.828	13	.910	31	.785
14	.922	32	.822	14	.903	32	.778
15	.917	33	.817	15	.896	33	.771
16	.911	34	.811	16	.889	34	.764
17	.906	35	.806	17	.882	35	.757
18	.900	36	.800	18	.875	36	.750

ments of $800 each). And that's not counting any earnings you may gain if you save some of the money. If you wait until you are 65, you will be 77 years old before the extra $200 a month adds up to $28,800 ($200 times 12 months times 12 years equals $28,800).

Social Security is there for you to take advantage of at age 62. But once you start taking benefits at that age, you cannot change your mind. If your new career has taken off and you are earning more than the maximum that Social Security allows, you could find yourself giving back to Social Security at the end of the year. And if your income is more than a certain level, up to one-half of your benefits could be taxed as ordinary income. You will need to look at your total picture before you make a final decision and notify Social Security. The following two sections talk about such earnings and the IRS.

What If You Earn Money While Getting Social Security?

It is OK to earn a certain amount, but if you earn more you pay a penalty. Earned money is what you get from wages or self-employment. Interest on your savings, dividends from investments, income from pensions, rental income from real estate—none of these counts as earned money. If you are under age 65, the limit you may earn is $7,440. If you've reached 65 and are not yet 70, the top is $10,200. Once you are 70, there is no limit on how much you may earn.

What's the penalty—or "take-back" (to use the Social Security Administration's jargon)? Social Security reduces your benefits by $1 for every $2 you earn if you are under 65, or by $1 for every $3 if you are 65 but not yet 70. The amount that Social Security permits you to earn without penalty increases every year. There has been talk of eliminating the penalty for those between 65 and 69, but it is estimated that it would cost the government $25 to $30 billion over a five-year period. In other words, don't hold your breath.

The IRS Wants Some

Until 1984, Social Security benefits were exempt from Federal income taxes. But now, depending on your level of income, up to one-half of your benefits may be taxed.

If you are single, none of your Social Security benefits will be subject to tax if the total of your adjusted gross income plus one-half of your Social Security benefits add up to less than $25,000. If you are filing a joint return, the top is $32,000. The taxable amount is the *lesser* of two items: either one-half of your Social Security benefits or one-half of the income that is more than $25,000 for single filers or $32,000 for joint filers.

Look at it this way: If your income (including pension, taxable interest income, nontaxable interest income, and one-half of your Social Security benefits) exceeds the above amounts, your Social Security benefits become taxable.

EXAMPLE: Suppose you and your spouse are receiving $15,000 in Social Security benefits during the current tax year. If one-half of that amount (i.e., $7,500) plus other gross income including tax-exempt interest totals less than $32,000, none of your Social Security benefits will be taxed. If, however, your total income is $35,000, you will be taxed on $1,500 (i.e., one-half of the amount above $32,000).

TIP: Watch for changes in the taxing of your Social Security benefits between now and the time of your retirement. Congress keeps looking for more sources of revenue. The portion of Social Security benefits subject to federal tax could rise from the present 50 percent to as high as 85 percent.

How about state income taxes on Social Security benefits? Some states tax them, some do not. So check on whether your state does. A state that has an income tax usually follows federal guidelines.

Keep an Eye on Social Security Changes

A lot of evolution has occurred in Social Security regulations over the past decade, and it has not stopped yet. One factor affecting the system is that the United States has become a debtor nation. Some time in the second decade of the twenty-first century, the amount being paid into the system by wage earners is expected to slip below the amount needed to pay benefits. That is when the surplus in the trust fund will have to be tapped. But if the surplus has been spent in the meantime to pay for day-to-day operations of the U.S. government, as the Treasury replaces cash with IOUs in the form of government bonds, how will the beneficiaries then

FACTS ABOUT YOUR SOCIAL SECURITY

January 26, 1990

THE FACTS
YOU GAVE US

Your Name .... **John Q. Public**
Your Social Security Number .... **XXX-XX-XXXX**
Your Date of Birth .... **December 16, 1947**
1989 Earnings **$25,376**
1990 Earnings **$26,000**
Your Estimated Future Average Yearly Earnings **$28,000**
The Age You Plan To Retire **62**

We used these facts and the information already on our records to prepare this statement for you. When we estimated your benefits, we included any 1989 and 1990 earnings and any future estimated earnings you told us about.

If you did not estimate your future earnings, we did not project any future earnings for you.

YOUR
SOCIAL
SECURITY
EARNINGS

The chart below shows the earnings on your Social Security record. It also estimates the amount of Social Security taxes you paid each year to finance benefits under Social Security and Medicare. We show earnings only up to the maximum amount of yearly earnings covered by Social Security. These maximum amounts are also shown on the chart. The chart may not include some or all of your earnings from last year because they may not have been posted to your record yet.

Years	Maximum Yearly Earnings Subject To Social Security Tax	Your Social Security Taxed Earnings	Estimated Social Security Taxes You Paid	Years	Maximum Yearly Earnings Subject To Social Security Tax	Your Social Security Taxed Earnings	Estimated Social Security Taxes You Paid
1937-1950	$3,000	$ 0	$ 0	1971	7,800	7,142	371
1951	3,600	0	0	1972	9,000	8,295	431
1952	3,600	0	0	1973	10,800	9,001	526
1953	3,600	0	0	1974	13,200	10,239	599
1954	3,600	0	0	1975	14,100	11,163	653
1955	4,200	0	0	1976	15,300	11,516	673
1956	4,200	0	0	1977	16,500	12,663	740
1957	4,200	0	0	1978	17,700	13,769	833
1958	4,200	0	0	1979	22,900	15,158	929
1959	4,800	0	0	1980	25,900	17,407	1,067
1960	4,800	0	0	1981	29,700	18,495	1,229
1961	4,800	0	0	1982	32,400	20,858	1,397
1962	4,800	0	0	1983	35,700	22,485	1,506
1963	4,800	0	0	1984	37,800	25,085	1,680
1964	4,800	632	22	1985	39,600	26,587	1,874
1965	4,800	497	18	1986	42,000	25,647	1,833
1966	6,600	3,607	151	1987	43,800	23,938	1,797
1967	6,600	4,053	178	1988	45,000	24,524	1,841
1968	7,800	3,833	168	1989	48,000	Not Yet Posted	
1969	7,800	5,282	253	1990	51,300		
1970	7,800	6,253	300				

YOUR
SOCIAL
SECURITY
CREDITS

To qualify for benefits, you need credit for a certain amount of work covered by Social Security. (See "How You Earn Social Security Credits" on the reverse side.) The number of credits you need will vary with the type of benefit. **Under current law, you do not need more than 40 credits to be fully insured for any benefit.**

Our review of your earnings, including any 1989 and 1990 earnings you told us about, shows that you now have **at least 40 Social Security credits.**

ESTIMATED BENEFITS

RETIREMENT
You must have **40** Social Security credits to be fully insured for retirement benefits. Assuming that you meet all the requirements, here are estimates of your retirement benefits based on your past and any projected earnings. The estimates are in today's dollars, but adjusted to account for average wage growth in the national economy.

If you retire at 62, your monthly benefit in today's dollars will be about .... **$ 815**

The earliest age at which you can receive an unreduced retirement benefit is **66 years of age.** We call this your full retirement age. If you wait until that age to receive benefits, your monthly benefit in today's dollars will be about **$1,090**

If you wait until you are 70 to receive benefits, your monthly benefit in today's dollars will be about **$1,445**

SURVIVORS
If you have a family, you must have **21** Social Security credits for certain family members to receive benefits if you were to die this year. They may also qualify if you earn 6 credits in the 3 years before your death. The number of credits a person needs to be insured for survivors benefits increases each year until age 62, up to a maximum of 40 credits.

Here is an estimate of the benefits your family could receive if you had enough credits to be insured, they qualified for benefits, and you died this year:

Your child could receive a monthly benefit of about .... **$ 675**

If your child and your surviving spouse who is caring for your child both qualify, they could each receive a monthly benefit of about .... **$ 675**

When your surviving spouse reaches full retirement age, he or she could receive a monthly benefit of about .... **$ 900**

The total amount that we could pay your family each month is about **$1,575**

We may also be able to pay your surviving spouse or children a one-time death benefit of .... **$ 255**

DISABILITY
Right now, you must have **21** Social Security credits to be insured for disability benefits. And, **20 of these** credits had to be earned in the **10 year period immediately before you became disabled.** If you are blind or received disability benefits in the past, you may need fewer credits. The number of credits a person needs to be insured for disability benefits increases each year until age 62, up to a maximum of 40 credits.

If you were disabled, had enough credits, and met the other requirements for disability benefits, here is an estimate of the benefits you could receive right now:

Your monthly benefit would be about .... **$ 895**

You and your eligible family members could receive up to a monthly total of about **$1,340**

IF YOU HAVE QUESTIONS
If you have any questions about this statement, please read the information on the reverse side. If you still have questions, please call **1-800-937-7005**. Social Security considers all calls confidential. We also want to ensure that you receive accurate and courteous service. That is why we have a second Social Security representative listen to some telephone calls.

be paid? The government might have to increase income taxes to cover the IOUs. Future recipients may find their Social Security benefits adjusted to compensate for an ever-increasing federal debt.

Don't Rely on the Government

What will happen in 2030 when 22 percent of the population will be over 65? That is twice the percentage in 1987. This figure alone tells you how important it is to start your own intensive saving and investing plan *now* if you plan to retire early. It is a MUST despite the added strain on your paycheck as Social Security taxes go up each and every year.

And if you are among those who enjoy a higher income now, don't rely on Social Security benefits to replace a substantial portion of that income. If you have consistently earned just about the maximum wage that is taxed by Social Security (e.g., $55,500 in 1992), your Social Security benefit at age 62 would replace about 23 percent of that income. If you are used to a $75,000 salary (again, in 1992), Social Security would pay you about 17 percent of that.

CHAPTER 7

Your Corporate Pension Plan

Your pension is the second leg of the three-legged stool of retirement. But pension benefits will probably not yet be available to you at the time when you kiss the rat race good-bye unless you are one of the fortunate people who are offered early retirement packages—or unless you manage to hold on until such a package is offered to you. What is important is for you to understand pensions, because you will have to make choices whenever you change jobs.

The idea of a company providing pensions is not all that old. A handful date from the turn of the century, but most have been established since about 1920, when fewer then 10 percent of employees worked for companies that provided such benefits. Furthermore, early pension plans were for office employees, not for blue-collar workers.

Attracting and Holding People

Pension plans didn't really become universal until a major expansion began, following the end of World War II in 1945. As the labor unions fought for pensions to supplement the small amount their members were getting from Social Security, companies quickly discovered that a solid pension plan could attract employees and help to keep them.

Yet there was a catch. Many people who retired in the 1960s and early 1970s had rude awakenings: The amount of pension benefit that they began to receive upon retirement was not as much as they had anticipated. Abuses were widespread—and usually in favor of the employer.

So Congress passed legislation: the Employee Retirement Income Security Act of 1974 (ERISA). It set rules about how pensions are funded, who is eligible for them, and how day-to-day operations must be conducted. It also prescribed minimum standards with which the plans it covers must comply.

One of ERISA's intentions was to put pensions in the American free enterprise system on a sound financial footing. To do this, it established the Pension Benefit Guaranty Corporation (PBGC) under the jurisdiction of the U.S. Department of Labor. Just as the purpose of the Federal Deposit Insurance Corporation (FDIC) is to protect the savings of depositors if banks fail, the PBGC guarantees benefits to pension-plan participants even if a plan's assets are insufficient to meet its obligations.

Variety of Pension Plans

Pension plans come in a wide variety. Let's look at some.

1. Defined Benefit Plan

This plan specifies (i.e., "defines") in advance the benefit that you will receive. Under the law, your company must fund such a plan in advance, to be sure the money will be available when you retire. The plan sets up a formula—usually based on your years of service and your annual pay in the last few years of your employment. Your employer is then required to put enough into this pension fund over the years so that the amount you receive will equal the amount prescribed by the formula. This type of plan is federally insured.

This plan counts on your employer to make a long-term commitment and bear a certain risk: The company must provide the level of retirement benefits that are guaranteed to you—that is, your employer must keep the promise of a specified amount for you when you retire—no matter what happens to the plan's investments or to the national economy.

EXAMPLE

Suppose your company formula is 1.5 percent of your average monthly earnings for your last five years of service, multiplied by your number of years of service. Say you figured on retiring at age 65, and you have final average earnings of $50,000 (at $4,167 per month). Your formula would be:

$$\$4,167 \times 1.5\% \times 30 \text{ years} = \$1,875 \text{ per month.}$$

If you had 15 years of service, the formula would produce $937 per month for you.

Some companies prefer to base the pension earnings on the entire time you participated in the plan. They average your earnings ("career-average earnings," they call it) and provide you with a certain percentage of that average.

EXAMPLE

Your pension may be based on 60 percent of your career-average earnings if you have worked for the company for 30 years. Then the company may add 1 percent for each year more than 30, or subtract 1 percent for each year under 30. Here's the catch: Your career-average earnings are almost certain to be less than the average for your last five years of service, because you were undoubtedly earning substantially less in your early years than you do today. Working for 30 years, you might have career-average earnings of $32,000, or $2,667 per month. At 60 percent, you'd get $1,600 in your monthly pension check. Using the formula that subtracts 1 percent for each year less than 30, if you had worked for just 15 years and had the *same* career average earnings you would get 15 percent less, or $1,360.

You should be aware that ERISA sets a dollar limit on the amount of annual benefit your company is allowed to pay you. The 1992 limit is $112,222, up from $98,064 in 1989. Because it is adjusted for the cost of living, the limit changes each year. Note also that the limit is based on retirement at age 65.

2. Defined Contribution Plan

Some companies call this one an *Individual Account Plan*. It allows the company to contribute a fixed amount, which can change each year, to an individual account that invests the money. Recently, many companies have decided to switch from defined benefit plans to defined contribution plans because they can limit their costs to the fixed annual contribution.

When your retirement starts, your pension benefit is then based on the amount accumulated in your individual account. The total that is waiting there, of course, depends on how well the plan's investments have performed.

WARNING! Some ground rules that you should understand about defined contribution plans:

1. Separate accounts are maintained for each employee. Investment gains and losses are posted to each individual account. That means that, unlike the defined benefit plan, the defined contribution plan can suffer losses. If they occur just before your retirement, you are the one who bears the risk and gets hurt.
2. Contributions are limited to $30,000 annually or 25 percent of your pay—whichever is less. This means that if you are earning $50,000, the annual contribution on your behalf cannot be more than $12,500.
3. This type of plan is not insured. It does not offer the same protection that a defined benefit plan provides.

A defined contribution plan may be set up as any one of the following:

• *Money Purchase Plan:* The amount of the contribution for each year is set by a predetermined formula, and is either a fixed dollar amount or a fixed percentage of your pay. Your employer *must* then make the contribution (under this plan, it is mandatory).

• *Profit-Sharing Plan:* Your employer's contribution may vary each year, depending on the company's profits. Usually, company contributions are divided among the participants in proportion to their respective earnings. Your company is under no obligation to make contributions on a regular (or even on an irregular) basis. Under this plan, contributions are *not* mandatory.

ANDY IS HEADING FOR HALF A MILLION: After working for his company for 23 years, Andy has $310,000 in a profit-sharing plan. The company has put in 15 percent of his salary each and every year. With his current income at $68,000, he now salts away more than $10,000 a year. Over the next several years, this will increase as he gets raises.

• *Employee Stock Ownership Plan (ESOP):* In recognition of your value to the company, your employers permit you to buy stock in the company (this plan often applies to a privately held company, not to a publicly held one). Your ESOP is required to invest primarily in such employer stock, and it is permitted to borrow money to buy the stock.

• *Voluntary Contribution Plans:* These, including the 401(k) plan and other thrift plans, are discussed in a subsequent chapter.

• *Multiple Plans:* Some companies offer more than one plan. For example, you may be offered a defined benefit plan as well as a defined contribution plan. If the plans are similar (e.g., two profit-sharing plans), they are treated as a single plan and total contributions are limited. If they are not similar (e.g., a profit-sharing plan and a defined benefit plan), the company must use a formula for each individual employee that keeps total contributions and benefits within certain limits.

Which are the most popular plans? The Employee Benefit Research Institute reports that the number of defined contribution plans has been increasing at a much faster rate than the number of defined benefit plans. Why? Changes in legislation and in the attitudes of employers as they shift more responsibility onto the employees.

Answers to Typical Questions

1. What is "vesting"?

When you are vested in your pension plan, you have the legal right to receive money from it even if you resign or are fired. How much you receive depends on how much both you and your employer have put in and how long you have been with the company.

Whatever you have put in is yours. So your actual contributions "vest" immediately. No one can take them away from you. But whatever your company puts in is subject to various conditions:

• *Cliff vesting* means that you get full benefits (i.e., everything in your account—your contributions plus your employer's contributions) after five years as an employee.

• *Partial vesting* means that after three years, in addition to whatever you have put in, you get 20 percent of whatever your employer has put in, and you gain another 20 percent in each of the next four years. Thus you are vested 100 percent at the end of seven years.

Not many years ago, an employee had to work for the company for anywhere from 10 to 14 years before becoming fully vested. If people changed jobs before they were fully vested, they lost all or a large percentage of the company's contribution to their pension plan. This helped keep down turnover, but times have changed. People move from job to job more often, and vesting requirements, especially since 1989, have changed to meet current conditions. As a result, more people are eligible for full pension money when they retire.

2. But What Happens to Vested Benefits If I Change Jobs?

If you are fully vested—that is, if you are entitled to your company's contributions as well as those you have made—that money is yours even if you quit or resign to take another job or are fired. Your particular company's plan may, however, specify whether you get the money immediately in a lump sum or must wait until you reach retirement age. Usually it depends on what kind of plan it is.

If it is a *defined benefit plan*, your vested benefits will probably be frozen at the time when you leave the company. You cannot get them until you become eligible for early retirement. You will then receive them as monthly income.

If it is a *defined contribution plan*, you will probably be paid your vested benefits in a lump sum when you depart. You can then roll the money over into an Individual Retirement Account (IRA). Or, depending on the policy of your new employer, you may find that the lump sum is "portable," meaning that you can roll it over into a qualified pension plan at your new job.

Note that if you choose the IRA, you will have to make your own investment decisions. If, on the other hand, you roll it over into the plan at your new job, your decisions will be limited to whatever investment programs your new company has to offer.

One thing more: If the company you are leaving freezes your pension money from the time you leave until the day you retire, you can expect inflation to erode some of it. How much, of course, depends on the annual rate of inflation multiplied by the number of years your pension money sits waiting for you to retire.

And a final point: If you change jobs often, working five years here and five years there, you will not be building up or accruing sizable pension benefits. Worth some hard thinking if you want to achieve financial independence in 10 to 15 years.

3. Who Gets the Benefits I Leave Behind?

If you leave your job before you are fully vested, you forfeit all or some of the money the company has put in—depending on whether your company has partial vesting or cliff vesting. Under a defined benefit plan, that left-behind money goes back into the total fund, helping to reduce the amount the company must put in. In a defined contribution plan, the forfeited funds may be used that way (i.e., to reduce the company's future contributions) or they may be shared by the employees whom you are leaving behind.

4. What Is a "Social Security Offset"?

Some companies feel that they should have some credit for the contributions they must make to Social Security every payday on your behalf. They view Social Security as your "second pension." So they integrate their company pension plan with Social Security, reducing your pension benefits a percentage of the amount of your Social Security check, or by a portion of it. This is a matter of company policy, decided on when the plan was set up.

EXAMPLE

Suppose your company uses a direct Social Security offset of 1.5 percent, multiplied by your years of service. If your monthly Social Security benefit is $1,000, your pension will be reduced by $450 (i.e., $1,000 multiplied by 1.5 percent multiplied by 30).

Your company may use an indirect offset. It may give you more pension benefits for your earnings above a certain level than it gives for those below that level. Usually the dividing line is the point where you have reached the maximum Social Security payments for the year and payroll deductions stop until the next January 1.

EXAMPLE

Such a formula might be: earnings on which the company paid Social Security multiplied by 1 percent multiplied by years of service, followed by earnings above Social Security maximum multiplied by 1.5 percent multiplied by years of service.

5. What If I Get Laid off Temporarily or Take a Leave of Absence?

What happens depends on how long you are out, and for what reason. In most plans, a break of less than one year in your record of service does not cost you any loss of vesting. If you are out for longer than one year, most plans make you go through a waiting period—usually a year—before you can get back into the plan. Maternity or paternity leave is different: Usually it is treated as if you were working full-time.

6. What about Cost-of-Living Adjustments?

Very few pensions are indexed for inflation. Not many companies offer automatic cost-of-living increases. So when you start receiving retirement benefits, what you see is likely to be what you get. Yet some companies have made increases in benefits from time to time when funds were available and they were concerned about their retirees. Better check on your company's policy.

7. What Happens If I Am Disabled Before I Retire?

Most plans pay full benefits if you become disabled. The benefits may, however, be tied to your age or years of service. A key point in determining whether you are eligible will be exactly what your disability is—how it is defined.

8. What If I Die Before Retiring?

Defined benefit plans will provide a death benefit to your spouse if you are vested and die before retiring. The benefit is paid as an annuity, starting on the date when you would have become eligible for early retirement. There is a catch in most plans: You must have been married for at least one year when you die. Defined contribution plan benefits would be paid to your spouse either as an annuity or in a lump sum.

Start Making Plans for the Money

As soon as you have an idea of when you will receive the money, it is important to start planning what you will do with it. You will have a number of options. Don't panic—but think of them as critical decisions, for you will be living with them for a long time.

The basic choice that you are most likely to have is between taking a lump-sum payment or receiving monthly checks from an annuity over a specified period.

Lump-Sum Distribution

If yours is a *defined contribution plan*, it will probably be paid out to you as a lump sum. This is relatively simple, for what is in the plan is the contributions that you and your company have each put in, plus the earnings and the gains and losses. The lump sum you can take out is determined by how much you are vested.

If you are in a *defined benefit plan* and it is paid out in a lump sum, the amount you get will be computed based on interest rates and mortality tables that are specified in the plan. In effect, an actuary (an insurance expert who calculates rates and premiums) will have to figure out how long you can expect to live and what rates of interest would be paid on the money if it were held over that period. The lump sum then must match the total amount that you would expect to receive over your lifetime if you were taking monthly payments rather than the lump sum.

HOW TO AVOID THE TAX BITE

If you take the money in a lump sum, you will have to decide whether to roll it over into an Individual Retirement Account (IRA), thus postponing paying taxes on it, or not roll it over and pay taxes on it.

If you take the money when you leave your company and do not roll it over into an IRA, it will be taxed as ordinary income in the year when you take it. You can soften that blow by doing five-year forward averaging on your income tax return, but only if you meet several qualifications:

1. You are at least 59 ½ years old. The only exception: If you reached age 50 before January 1, 1986, but have not yet reached 59 ½, you may take advantage of five-year forward averaging.

2. You have been a participant in your plan for at least five years before receiving the lump-sum distribution.

3. You use the special averaging for *all* lump-sum amounts you receive in the taxable year.

4. If you are covered by more than one qualified plan, you receive the full balance of all the plans of the same type. (For example, suppose you had an earlier job where you were fully vested and your employer froze your pension money when you left, so that it has been waiting for your retirement; you would take it now, if it can be taken as a lump sum, and add it to your total for forward averaging. You would have to withdraw the proceeds from both plans.)

5. The lump sum is being paid to you because you no longer work for the company that sponsors the plan. You must be "separated from service" for your money to qualify as a lump-sum distribution.

6. Once you take advantage of five-year forward averaging, you may not do so again, no matter what lump-sum distributions you may get in the future.

TWO IMPORTANT POINTS to remember: 1) When you do five-year forward averaging, the Internal Revenue Service considers you to be a single person who claims no exemptions—whether or not you are married or have dependents. The tax on your lump sum is calculated separately, without consideration of any other income. This results in a lower tax than if your lump sum were included with your other income. 2) If you are younger than 59½, you will have to pay the ordinary income tax on your lump sum.

WHAT'S THE BEST BET?

There can be good reasons for taking your lump-sum distribution as cash rather than rolling it over. If you are aiming for financial independence, you may need the money to set up your own business, or to buy income-producing real estate, or for any number of reasons. Or you may need it because of a health problem—yours or someone else's. Under the circumstances, you just have to swallow hard and pay the taxes.

Think about it. And think about the fact that the Employee Benefit Research Institute reports that more than one-half of today's workers who take the lump sums from their pensions or from tax-deferred savings accounts do not save or invest the money. They spend it. And when it is gone, it is gone.

The key words for you are *financial independence*. If you are under 59½ and if you do not absolutely *need* the money, your best bet is to roll it over into an IRA. You get 60 days to decide—60 days from the date when you receive the money. Then, once it is in your IRA, you pay no taxes on it until you start making withdrawals.

INVESTMENT DECISIONS, TOO

You not only have to decide about your tax situation. You must also decide where to put the money. One of the important reasons for taking the lump-sum distribution in the first place is that you keep control of the money. You make all the decisions on investments.

Rolling it over into an IRA gives you great flexibility in investments. Many different kinds of investments are available, and you can divide the money among several different "vehicles." (An investment "vehicle" is not a method of transportation that rolls on wheels; it is a type of savings or investment account in a bank or mutual fund or individual stocks and bonds.) You can also switch investments later as your needs, or market conditions, change.

Table 5. Lump-Sum Distribution:
5-Year Averaging versus Rollover

$100,000 Lump-Sum Distribution versus IRA Rollover		
	Lump-Sum Distribution	IRA Rollover
5-Year Averaging Tax:	$ 15,000	N/A
Amount Available to Invest	85,000	$100,000
Accumulated Value—5 years	108,484[a]	146,933[b]
Accumulated Value—10 years	138,456[a]	215,892[b]
$200,000 Lump-Sum Distribution versus IRA Rollover		
	Lump-Sum Distribution	IRA Rollover
5-Year Averaging Tax:	$ 42,733	N/A
Amount Available to Invest	157,227	$200,000
Accumulated Value—5 years	200,666[a]	293,866[b]
Accumulated Value—10 years	256,106[a]	431,785[b]
$250,000 Lump-Sum Distribution versus IRA Rollover		
	Lump-Sum Distribution	IRA Rollover
5-Year Averaging Tax:	$ 56,878	N/A
Amount Available to Invest	193,122	$250,000
Accumulated Value—5 years	246,478[a]	367,332[b]
Accumulated Value—10 years	314,575[a]	539,731[b]

[a] Funds are invested tax-free at a 5% rate of return. Though the funds could be invested for a higher rate of return in a taxable investment, income taxes would be due each year on the interest and dividends that the money earned. The accumulated value, therefore, at the end of the period might be the same. (See chapter 10 on saving and investing for taxable versus tax-free equivalents.)

[b] Funds are invested at an 8% rate of return. At the end of the five- or ten-year period, the money may be withdrawn in a single lump sum, paying income taxes on the full amount, or annually, paying income taxes only on the amount withdrawn.

SOURCE: Dworken, Hillman, LaMorte & Sterczala, PC

A COUPLE OF TIPS:

• You may risk losing some other employee benefits if you take a lump-sum distribution. Some companies, for instance, stop medical coverage on employees who retire and take their pension money with them, whereas they maintain coverage on retirees who leave the money in the company's hands and accept monthly retirement pay. Check your company's policy before you make final decisions.

• If you're between jobs, you can park your lump-sum distribution in a rollover IRA until you have a new job where you can shift it into the new employer's qualified retirement plan— *if they allow you to do so.* Important: Keep this money in its own separate IRA. Do not commingle it with other IRA money, or you will not be allowed to move the lump sum from your earlier company into your new company's retirement plan. Nor will you be able to use the special income forward-averaging in the future. *You must keep lump sums separate unto themselves.*

What if you withdraw money from a rollover IRA? It follows the same rules that apply if you make a withdrawal from an IRA that you yourself set up (see p. 135).

Annuity

An annuity is a fixed annual payment. Usually it is paid monthly. Once it is set up and you are committed to it, there is—at least in most cases—no turning back.

All defined benefit plans offer you the option of setting up an annuity. Some also offer you lump-sum distribution.

WHO MAKES THE RIGHT GUESS?

The advantage of an annuity is that it protects you against the possibility of living too long, for it guarantees that you will be paid your fixed monthly income as long as you live. You cannot outlive your payments.

If you are not too confident about handling money, and if you want the security of knowing that a check will arrive each month (or a direct deposit will be made to your bank account each month), an annuity may well be best for you.

But you should be aware of certain disadvantages:

1. Inflation can erode your annuity's value. Your monthly payment stays the same, no matter what inflation does—unless yours is one of the rare companies that provide a cost-of-living adjustment. Some companies offer periodic increases in payments even though they are under no obligation to do so. An inflation rate of only 3 percent, which is quite modest, means that your fixed monthly payment could lose about one-third of its purchasing power in 11 years.

2. You cannot change your mind. Once you have selected your annuity, you must live with your decision.

3. Payments end when you die (except for joint-and-survivor annuities—see table 6). If you retire today, put $50,000 into an annuity tomorrow, and drop dead the next day, your heirs get nothing. And, as one joker put it, "The insurance company throws a big party." If, on the other hand, you live far longer than the actuaries ever thought you would, it will be the insurance company that made the wrong guess . . . and that keeps on paying you.

JOINT-AND-SURVIVOR ANNUITIES

A law passed in 1984 protects your spouse from losing everything if you start to take payments from an annuity and die before your spouse dies. It created a *50 percent joint-and-survivor annuity*. If you die before your spouse, this automatically pays your spouse 50 percent of the amount you were being paid. Payments continue as long as your spouse then lives. If you decide you don't want, or don't need, this feature, you and your spouse must both sign a waiver and have it notarized. You can also choose from other options:

• *Straight Life Annuity.* This provides the highest monthly payment directly to you for the rest of your life. When you die, it ends. Nothing is provided for your spouse. This one is worth considering only if your spouse will also be receiving a pension, or is in such poor health that he or she is not expected to survive you, or if you have substantial life insurance already in place.

• *10-Year Certain.* Under this arrangement, payments are paid to you for your lifetime and are guaranteed to a beneficiary if you should die within the 10 years. The same kind of annuity can be set up for 15 or 20 years, but paying proportionately less each month, of course. *Warning*: If you live longer than the "period certain," your beneficiary will get no payments.

• *Other Joint-and-Survivor Annuities.* If you prefer to have your survivor get more than 50 percent of the amount you are receiving—say, 75 or 100 percent—you can set it up that way. Obviously, the monthly payments in this annuity must be smaller than in the others, because the total amount is being spread more widely.

Some financial advisers say, "Take the straight life option. Then buy a life insurance policy for your spouse, in case you die first." They call this "pension max." But be careful. Two points to check on: (1) How much insurance will you need in order to provide after-tax income that is equivalent to the benefits your spouse will get if he or she survives you? (2) What if the insurance company's investments don't perform as well as projected and you find yourself paying a higher premium for the same coverage? If the insurance becomes too expensive, you might then have to cut back the amount of coverage or let the policy lapse. That would leave your spouse without the very benefit the 50 percent joint-and-survivor annuity would have provided. On top of that, remember, the insurance benefit will not grow to keep pace with inflation. Your pension *might* have cost-of-living increases built in for the benefit of your spouse. Suppose your retirement plan were paid out as a straight-life annuity, and you expected $50,000 a year. Here are the actual payments you would get under various joint-and-survivor options, and in a 10-year certain payout.

Table 6. Annuity Payments

Employee Age	Spouse Age	50% J&S	75% J&S	100% J&S	10-Year Certain
		Annual Benefit: $50,000			
55	52	$45,800	$43,950	$42,245	$48,387
60	57	44,835	42,635	40,640	47,309
65	62	43,760	41,185	38,400	45,556

SOURCE: The Wyatt Company

HOW YOUR ANNUITY IS TAXED

If your employer provided all of your pension money, you must report the monthly payments you get as ordinary income. But if you contributed to the plan, part of each payment you get is tax free and part is taxable. The IRS provides tables on calculating the taxable portion.

Things to Think about in Lump Sum or Annuity

One of your first questions is bound to be: How safe is my pension money? Aside from the fact that you will almost certainly get your vested pension funds when you retire, the situation is fraught with possible dangers. You have no guarantee that you will collect other fringe benefits (e.g., companies that have promised their retirees such fringe benefits as major medical insurance and annual check-ups have, in many cases, reneged).

Pensions are usually put into trust funds where they are protected from the company's creditors if the company goes into bankruptcy. Your employer is required by law to pay premiums to the Pension Benefit Guaranty Corporation (PBGC) on behalf of each employee who is in a defined benefit plan, thus buying coverage if the company's plan fails before benefits are paid. (Actually, if your company's plan is fully funded or overfunded, as are about 80 percent of all plans, your benefits are secure.)

As a federal agency created to make good on shortfalls when pension plans run out of money, PBGC guarantees pensions only up to $27,000 a year. If your pension is to be larger than that, you run the risk of possibly not getting every penny. As for defined contribution plans, such as profit-sharing or 401(k), the PBGC does not guarantee them.

Some Things to Be Aware Of

• Your company cannot take away your vested benefits. It cannot set back its early retirement date. But it can change its pension formula for future years. If it should adopt a less generous formula, you could end up with less than you have been counting on.

• A number of companies are ending their defined benefit plans and setting up defined contribution plans instead. When it was obligated to pay a stated amount of benefits under the defined benefit plan, the company bore all of the risk of investing. Under the defined contribution plan, the company shifts the risk to the employee. If your company does this, *you* have to make decisions about investments.

• The pension fund manager working with the defined benefit plan probably used an investment strategy that was growth oriented. The annuities now bought under the defined contribution plan will be fixed-income investments. Lacking growth potential, they will not be able to keep up with inflation. Result: Younger workers whose pensions evolve under this changed policy may very well end up with smaller retirement funds than older employees who retire soon.

• Another worrisome factor is the financial health of the insurance companies from which the annuities are bought. A pension fund manager wants to be sure of his or her insurance companies. Not every insurer has been solid and stable in recent years.

• Then there are mergers and takeovers. If your employer sells out to a company with a plan that is less generous than yours, your pension is threatened. Suppose, for example, you are working for a company that provides unreduced pension benefits for an employee with 30 years of service at age 55. Now suppose your company is acquired by a company that pays unreduced benefits only to employees over 60 years old. If you are 53 and have been expecting to retire in two years at 55, you are in for a rude awakening . . . and for not two but seven more years on the job before you can claim your pension.

Get an Estimate Now

The pension administrator in your company can work up an estimate of your retirement benefits at various ages and under both the single and joint-and-survivor options. Good idea to ask for that today, to help you begin to get a complete understanding of your pension. You don't want any surprises when you give notice that you're leaving. Put the estimate in your retirement file, and get it updated at least every couple of years so you will know of any changes in policy that may affect you.

What's the best way to insure your future pension benefits? Join a company with a good solid pension plan—and stay with it. Thirty years with one company will give you much better benefits than you can hope to get by working four or five years for each of five or six different companies.

What Is the Effect of Retiring *Really* Early?

The retirement age in most plans is 65. But the usual plan also provides retirement benefits to any employee who satisfies certain requirements—usually either age or age-and-service requirements. (For example, a typical teacher contract permits retirement with full benefits when any combination of your age and your years of service adds up to 75.) Generally speaking, the minimum at which you can "officially" retire in most companies is 55. If you plan to retire younger than 65, the plan almost always reflects two key elements: (1) the shorter length of your employment, which means that not as many payday contributions will be made by you and/or your employer, and (2) the longer time that benefits will have to be paid to you after you retire.

The estimate of retirement benefits at different ages that you get from your pension administrator will show you how much less you will get for retiring in each year younger than 65.

Working longer, then, increases your pay for purposes of gaining pension benefits. It also increases your assets, as you continue to put away savings or to make long-term investments. So it is important to think about what you are giving up when you head for early retirement, and to plan on compensating for it.

Now let's take a look at the effect that retiring early can have on the amount you will receive in pension benefits. It's a good idea to understand this right now, so you won't have any nasty surprises when you want to kiss the rat race good-bye.

Suppose you started working for a company when you were 30, and the company's pension program is a defined benefit plan. If you wait until you reach 65 to retire, you will get full benefits. The formula for your pension will be your years of service times the average of your last five years of salary times 1.5 percent. You are making a good salary now, and you expect to get an annual increase of at least 5 percent. That means you could be making $100,000 or more by the time you reach 65. If at that time your average pay for the last five years comes out at $96,000, your annual pension will be about $50,500.

Early retirement is usually defined as age 55. That is, the company will pay out pension benefits at that age, but with a reduced amount. Some companies offer full benefits if you have the right combination of age and years of service. For instance, Ken and Shelley were able to collect their pensions at age 50 because they had been with the school system for 25 years. For them, the minimum requirement was a formula that said any combination of age and years of service that totaled 75 was acceptable. If you leave your company before you are entitled to full benefits, you may be able to get a lump-sum payment that you can roll over into an IRA, or the benefits may be frozen until you reach early retirement age (see p. 74).

You have no intention of staying until you reach 65. For each year before 65 that you do not stay (starting at age 55), the com-

RETIREMENT PENSION: Effect of Early Retirement

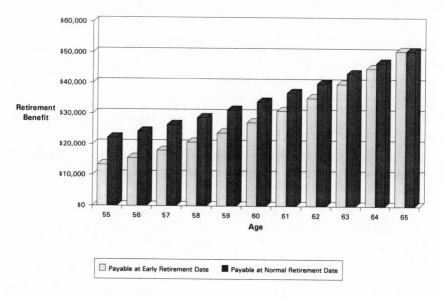

SOURCE: The Wyatt Company

pany will reduce your benefit by, say, 4 percent. That means that if you retire at 55, for instance, and start taking pension payments at that time, your annual pension will be about $13,300.

What are the chances of your staying with the same company for 30 or more years? Probably very slim. Then how will this affect your pension money?

Suppose you started to work for Company A when you were 30, and you stayed 5 years, with a final average pay of $22,200. Then, at Company B you stayed 13 years and your final average pay was $42,000. At Company C, after another 16 years, you reached age 65 and your final average earnings were $96,000 (the same final five-year average as we used in the example above, where you stayed with the same company for more than 35 years).

Your pension benefits from Company A would be about $3,300, and from Company B, $8,200—both payable at age 65. If you stayed with Company C to age 65, your benefits there would be

RETIREMENT PENSION: Benefit Payable at Early Retirement Date

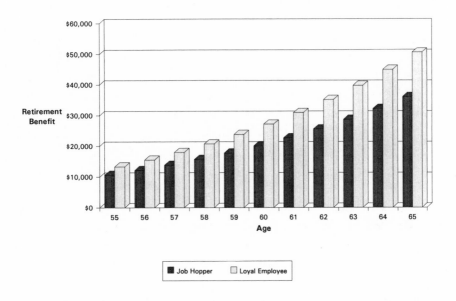

SOURCE: **The Wyatt Company**

roughly $24,500. That's a total benefits package, from all three companies, of about $36,000.

But you decided not to stay until you reached 65. If you left Company C when you were 55, your benefits would be reduced. Your annual payment, starting at 55, would be about $10,600 (see the chart on this page.)

So They're Offering You an Early Retirement Package

You think your job is perfectly safe. Then someone opens a "window." You're not supposed to jump out of it—you are supposed to take advantage of it. For the company's benefit. And for your own benefit.

The formal name is "early retirement incentive package." The "window" is because you get only a limited time to take advantage of it. What's it all about?

It's an idea whose time came in the late 1980s. In 1987, only one-third of the Fortune 1000 companies were regularly offering "buyouts" to their older employees. Then management caught hold of the idea that they could trim staffs and reduce payrolls, in effect clearing out the highly paid older people, without actually firing them—by offering them fairly irresistible incentives to retire. By 1990, 60 percent of the big companies were offering such packages.

This could be a blessing if you are planning to get out of the corporate rat race early. But it can be a mixed blessing because, if you decide to hold out for such a deal, you might have to wait until you are 55. Generally speaking, about two-thirds of such packages are not offered until age 55. Such a package is seldom offered to anyone under 50. Rather, a straight severance package is presented. It offers little choice.

If you are offered an early retirement incentive package, the "window" is the limited period you are given in which to decide whether to take the company up on the deal. Usually it is from 30 to 90 days.

The tough part is that you have no way of knowing exactly what may happen if you do not take it. If the company offers early retirement to a number of people and doesn't get enough who accept, it may decide to make some involuntary layoffs. Or, if you do stay on at work, you may have to settle for a lesser job.

How Voluntary Is Voluntary?

To help with your decision, do some research. How widespread is the offer? Is it to all employees who are 55 or older, with at least 10 years of service? Or is it limited to one department, or one plant, or certain individuals? The more widespread, the less your chance of being laid off if you do not accept. The more limited, the more likely you will be laid off. If the deal is being targeted to individuals, you'd better take it.

The package may be complicated. Study it. How does it compare to what you would get over the years if you stayed until normal retirement age? Or to what you would get if you were laid off after not taking it?

What should you be looking for when you study the offer?

1. *Pension benefits.* The incentive package should include an upward adjustment that gives you greater pension benefits than you would have expected if you simply retired early on your own. For example, suppose you retired at age 55 *without* the incentive package. You might have to pay a penalty, receiving 5 percent less for each year of retirement before you reach 65. But the incentive package may reduce or eliminate that penalty. The company may even add years of service and age to enhance your record. For instance, in what is known as a "five and five," the company would add five years to your length of service and five years to your age for the purpose of calculating your benefits. So if you are 55 with 20 years of service, you would be considered 60 with 25 years. Or your company might offer a "three and three."

IMPORTANT: When you ponder all this, remember that the pension calculations are based on your current salary. They do not take into account any salary increases that you might have received if you had stayed on and the package had not been offered.

2. *Severance pay.* If you are 50 to 55, or older, you may be offered both pension enhancement and a severance deal. The common formula for severance is a week's to a month's pay for each year worked. Look also for "bridge" payments that tide you over until Social Security starts paying you when you are 62.

If you are under 50, the incentive package is likely to be straight severance pay—either a lump sum, or continued salary for a certain period.

3. *Medical coverage.* This is extremely important. If you accept the package, will you continue to be covered by the company medical plan, at least until you reach 65—at the same cost to you? Don't forget, an individual policy will cost you anywhere from $2,000 to $4,000 a year—and even more if it covers your spouse and your family.

4. *Pension payment.* How will your pension be paid? Some companies offer a lump sum, but most—80 to 90 percent of Fortune 1000 companies, for example—insist that you take an annuity. It starts when you accept the package, and it continues for the rest of your life. Unless it has a built-in cost-of-living adjustment, the amount is fixed permanently.

If you get a lump sum, you can roll it over into an Individual Retirement Account (IRA). If, however, you are under age 59 ½ when you get it, and if you need to use some of the money, you must understand the rules on early withdrawals from an IRA. See chapter 9 on the 10 percent penalty and payment of income tax on early withdrawals and on ways to avoid the penalties.

5. *Counseling services.* Some companies include career counseling and financial planning services when they offer early retirement incentive packages. Each of these is well worth the time you will spend with it, so take full advantage of whatever is offered.

TIP: You will probably find that your company is willing to negotiate over many points in the early retirement package it offers. If continuing medical coverage is not offered as part of the deal, you should definitely negotiate for it. And, depending on your position in the company, you may be able to bargain for additional years of service and for such specifics as payment of legal fees that you may incur.

So you've been offered an early retirement package. As an enhancement, the company is adding five years of service and five years of age. If you are 55 and have 25 years of service, for pension purposes they will consider you to be 60 with 30 years of service.

Look at the example on page 88. As you will recall, about $50,500 would be paid to you at age 65 if you had 35 years of service, while you would get about $13,300 if you retired at 55 and started taking benefits then. With the "five and five" enhancement, you would receive about $21,200 in benefits starting at age 55, or about $40,000 if the package were offered when you were 60.

As you study these graphs, remember that there is going to be

RETIREMENT PENSION: Effect of Early Retirement

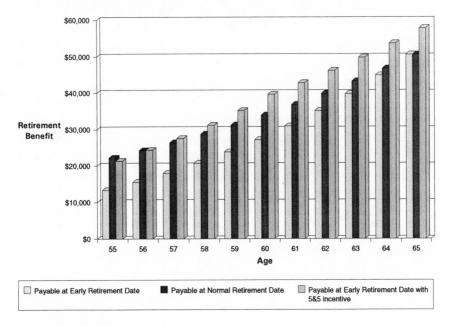

SOURCE: The Wyatt Company

a period of time before your pension and Social Security kick in, and there is bound to be a gap between the total they will provide and the amount you will want for a comfortable retirement. How much of a gap? Let's examine it closely in the next chapter.

Two Photographers in Retirement

Marvin was the principal of a New York City school. Ted worked for a major manufacturer. Marvin was a top-notch amateur photographer. Ted worked with the camera, and in the darkroom, every day as part of his job. Marvin was reaching burnout when he decided to leave the school system. Ted's company was cutting back when it decided to offer him—a company man for 37 years— an early retirement package.

Marvin looked forward to early retirement. Ted was furious— the company could relocate him if he decided not to accept the package, and could reduce his salary by two levels (i.e., back to where he was two raises ago). He took the package.

Today both of them are content. Marvin has become an accomplished photographer, winning awards and traveling as far away as China and Portugal on photographic safaris. He has also taken classes in Hebrew and tap dancing, does the cooking during the week (his wife is still working), and replies, if you ask him what he does in retirement, "Whatever I want to do." Ted has established a business as a free-lance photographer, and says he feels "like a 20-year-old again." Instead of getting home late and reheating dinner in the microwave, he is there, as his wife says, "listening to the birds and the rustle of the leaves, sitting on the deck he built. It's quite a change from the anger I saw when the company asked Ted to retire."

WORKSHEET VII: OUR PENSION PLANS

	Self	Spouse
1. Type of Plan	_____	
Defined Benefit	_____	
Defined Contribution	_____	
Profit-sharing	_____	
Money Purchase	_____	
401(k)	_____	
Other	_____	
2. Our Dollar Contribution to the Plan	_____	
3. Vesting	_____	
Full and Immediate	_____	
Gradual	_____	
5-Year (Cliff)	_____	
Years to Go until Vested	_____	
4. Years of Service to Date	_____	
5. Benefits		
Formula for Calculating Retirement Benefits	_____	
Amount of Social Security Offset, If Any	_____	
Get Credit for Working beyond Normal Retirement Age?	_____	
6. Requirements for Early Retirement	_____	
Number of Years of Service	_____	
Age	_____	
Percentage of Reduction for Each Year of Early Retirement	_____	
7. How Benefits Are Paid	_____	
Lump Sum	_____	
Annuity—Payment per Month	_____	

WORKSHEET VII: OUR PENSION PLANS (cont.)

     Joint-and-Survivor 50%   _____

     Joint-and-Survivor 75%   _____

     Joint-and-Survivor 100%   _____

     Life Certain   _____

     Straight Life   _____

     Cost-of-Living Adjustment?   _____

8. Benefits to Spouse If Employee
     Dies before Retirement   _____

9. Other Benefits Frozen at Earlier
     Employers (List)   _____
     Projected Value at Retirement _____

10. Pension Money Rolled over from
     Previous Employers into IRAs _____
     How Many?   _____
     Value of Each   _____

11. Notes or Questions to Ask Pension
     Administrator or Others   _____

CHAPTER 8

Filling the Gap

If you kiss the rat race good-bye before you have pension and Social Security benefits, where is your income going to come from?

At first, income from your savings and investments and from your new career must fill that gap. That is why it is so important for you to accumulate capital between now and the time when you want to be financially independent. The sooner you start, the more attainable your goal of living comfortably at a relatively young age—much younger than most people. Then once your pension and Social Security are available, you will be less dependent on income from your assets and from your new career.

This chapter concentrates on two worksheets. Worksheet VIII will help you estimate how much you will need in savings at the time when you stop working for others. Worksheet IX will help you decide how much you need to save each year until then.

For worksheet VIII, you will need figures from Social Security (see p. 20). Although you won't be getting Social Security yet at the time you become financially independent, it will be a source of income when you reach age 62 or whenever you are ready to retire officially. For that reason, it is important to look at how it will fit into your total financial picture.

If you have had several different employers, you may have several pensions. If your pension at any of them was frozen, get in touch and ask for an estimate of the amount of income you can expect and the age at which it begins. IMPORTANT: Do not in-

Table 7. Life Expectancy Table

At Age	Average Remaining Years		
	Male	Female	Combined Average
30	42.8	47.4	45.1
35	38.7	45.0	41.8
40	33.8	38.2	36.0
45	29.6	35.5	32.5
50	25.5	29.6	27.5
55	21.7	25.5	23.6
60	18.2	21.7	19.9
65	14.5	18.8	16.6
70	12.1	15.0	13.5
75	9.6	12.1	10.8
80	7.5	9.6	8.5
85	5.7	7.5	6.6

clude on this worksheet any amounts that you took with you when you left a company and that were rolled over into Individual Retirement Accounts (IRAs).

How's Your Crystal Ball?

How long will you be in retirement?

Crazy question! Who knows? Worksheet VIII asks you to take a serious, educated guess. In a matter like this, it is best to be conservative. Think about your state of health. Think about your genes—are you walking around carrying the genes of grandparents on either side or, even better, on *both* sides, who lived in good health well into their eighties? The Internal Revenue Service's table of life expectancy assumes that a 50-year-old male will live another 25.5 years—to age 75.5. Maybe you should add 10 years to that. Good idea: Check table 7 for your life expectancy.

Start filling in worksheet VIII; look at the sample worksheet

starting on page 101. When you come to line 4—Inflation Adjustment Factor—if your pension includes an annual cost-of-living adjustment (COLA), simply put "1" on the line. But check on this,
because most pensions do not include COLAs. If yours does *not*,
look at table 8: Inflation Adjustment for Pensions. And make another guess. What will inflation be? For example, if you expect to
live for 30 years in retirement and you expect inflation to stay at
about 4 percent, the inflation adjustment factor to put on line 4 is
.576.

Next, see table 9: Retirement Income Factors. If you expect 30
years of retirement living with inflation at 4 percent, put 17.29 on
line 8—Retirement Income Factor.

Work the numbers down. Line 9 tells you the savings you will
need when you retire. NOTE: The assumption is that all savings
will be tax deferred.

Now turn to worksheet IX to figure out how much you must
save each year in order to reach the savings you need to have when
you retire. To compile the figure you need for line 1, check your
data-gathering worksheets or your net worth statement in chapter
3. Note that line 1 asks for amounts saved on a tax-deferred basis.
Line 1 is also where you include any amounts that were rolled over
into IRAs when you left previous employers. You need to adjust
the figure for line 2 taking into consideration only inflation—see
table 10. The taxes are deferred until you start withdrawals. For
example, if you estimate a 9 percent rate of return and 4 percent
inflation, use 5 percent as a real rate of return.

Your compilation of investments on line 3, however, must be
adjusted for taxes as well as inflation. For example, if you think
you will earn 9 percent on your investments, and if your tax bracket
is 28 percent, it might be a good idea to take off three percentage
points for taxes. Again, see table 10. That's in addition to the 4
percent you deducted for the estimated rate of inflation. A return
of 9 percent, less inflation and taxes, will give you a real rate of
return of 2 percent.

Moving down worksheet IX, use table 11 to provide the Assumed

Discount Factor to enter on line 6. That number, times the amount still needed for early retirement (see line 5), will give you the annual savings you need for retirement. But don't forget to use line 8 to subtract the total amount of contributions coming from your employer—through your 401(k) plan, profit sharing, and ESOP. Line 9 then gives you the annual savings you will actually need.

Look at the difference tax deferral makes. Fifteen thousand dollars on a tax-deferred basis will have a value of $31,200 in 15 years, while the same amount on a taxable investment will give you one-third less, or $20,250. See the example worksheets on pages 101 to 104.

Now you know how much you need to save each year. *This* year is the time to start putting your savings and investment plan into action. To fill in the gap as much as possible, take advantage of every tax-deferred plan available, especially those to which your employer contributes. You'll get a higher rate of return from the tax-deferred plans. But if you still see some gaposis (i.e., if the gap is not entirely closed), see what after-tax investments you can make to help fill it in.

Are the bottom-line numbers on these two worksheets impossible to meet? Rethink. Refigure. Plan for retirement a few years later. Or plan for a lower annual income in retirement.

IMPORTANT! Don't forget that a worksheet is just that—a worksheet. Its purpose is to help you see how things stand so you can make comparisons, think things over, look at other possibilities. And the figures you have just gone through do not take into consideration future salary increases, returns on investments, inflation, additional contributions from your employer, or other changes that can affect, mostly in positive ways, your plan to retire early. Nor do these figures include your earnings from your new career.

One thing more. Rework your worksheets every year. That is very important. An outdated worksheet is useless. And don't put it off each year. Set yourself a deadline that is as absolute as the IRS deadline of April 15 for income-tax returns. If you procrastinate—well, procrastination is, to put it mildly, very costly.

WORKSHEET VIII: FILLING THE GAP:
TOTAL SAVINGS NEEDED

	Age Expected to Retire	Estimated Years in Retirement	Estimated Years to Retirement
Husband	*50*	*30*	*15*
Wife			

Estimated Inflation Rate __*4%*__
Estimated Rate of Return __*9%*__

1. Desired Gross Annual Income
   (Use 70 to 80% of present income.)
   Husband _____
   Wife   _____   *42,000*

2. Estimated Annual Social Security Benefit
   (Amount you would receive if retiring this year)
   Husband *13,000*
   Wife   *6,500*   *19,500*

3. Estimated Annual Income from Defined Benefit
   Plan(s) at Anticipated Retirement Date
   Husband 1 _____   2 *16,000*   *16,000*
   Wife   1 _____   2 _____   _____

4. Inflation Adjustment Factor—Table 8
   (Inflation Adjustment for Pension without COLA)
   Husband __*.576*__
   Wife   _____

5. Inflation Adjusted Pension Income
   (Line 3 times Line 4)
   Husband *.576* × *16,000*
   Wife   _____ × _____   *9,216*

6. Annual Income from Social Security
   and Pension
   (Line 2 plus Line 5)   *28,716*
   Husband _____
   Wife   _____

WORKSHEET VIII: FILLING THE GAP:
TOTAL SAVINGS NEEDED (cont.)

7. Additional Income Required
    (Line 1 minus Line 6)   13,284
    Husband _____
    Wife   _____

8. Retirement Income Factor—Table 9
    (Estimated Years in Retirement and Inflation
    Factor)
    Husband 17.29
    Wife   _____

9. Savings Required at Retirement Date
    (Line 7 times Line 8)   229,680
    Husband 17.29 × 13,284
    Wife   _____ × _____

WORKSHEET IX: FILLING THE GAP:
SAVINGS NEEDED PER YEAR

1. Amount Already Saved on Tax-Deferred Basis
   Include amounts in IRAs, profit-sharing plans,
   401(k)s, Keoghs, SEPs, cash value of life insurance.
   Husband *15,000*
   Wife   _____

2. Value at Retirement (See Table 10: Estimated
   Rates of Return)
   (Estimated rate of return less inflation, based on
   years to retirement.)
   Husband *2.08* × *15,000* = *31,200*
   Wife   _____ × _____ = _____   *31,200*

3. Amounts Already Saved in Non-Tax-Deferred
   Investments
   Include amounts in savings, CDs, stocks, bonds,
   mutual funds, equity in rental real estate (not your
   principal residence).
   Husband _____
   Wife   _____
   Joint   *15,000*

4. Value at Retirement (See Table 10: Estimated
   Rates of Return times Line 4)
   (Estimated rate of return less inflation and income
   taxes, based on years to retirement.)
   Husband _____ × _____ = _____
   Wife   _____ × _____ = _____
   Joint   *1.35* × *15,000* = *20,250*   *20,250*

5. Amount Still Needed for Retirement   _____
   Line 9 on worksheet VIII minus
   Line 2 and Line 4   *178,230*
   Husband _____
   Wife   _____

WORKSHEET IX: FILLING THE GAP:
SAVINGS NEEDED PER YEAR (cont.)

6. See Table 11: Assumed Discount Rate
(Estimated rate of return less inflation (and taxes if
saving on after-tax basis), based on years to
retirement.)
Husband __.049__
Wife   _____
7. Annual Savings Required for Retirement
Line 6 times Line 5
Husband _.049_ × _178,230_ = _8,733_
Wife   _____ × _____ = _____   _8,733_
8. Annual Employer Contribution to 401(k), Profit
Sharing, ESOP, Etc.
Husband _1,800_
Wife   _____   _1,800_
9. Annual Savings Needed
Line 7 minus Line 8
Husband _____
Wife   _____   _6,633_

Table 8. Inflation Adjustment for Pensions

Rate of Inflation (%)	Years of Retirement								
	5	10	15	20	25	30	35	40	45
4	.890	.811	.741	.679	.624	.576	.533	.494	.460
5	.865	.772	.691	.623	.563	.512	.467	.428	.394
6	.842	.736	.647	.573	.511	.458	.414	.376	.343
7	.820	.702	.607	.529	.466	.413	.369	.333	.302
8	.798	.671	.570	.490	.426	.375	.332	.298	.269

Table 9. Retirement Income Factors

Investment Return Adjusted for Inflation (%)	Years of Retirement								
	5	10	15	20	25	30	35	40	45
1	4.85	9.47	13.86	18.04	22.02	25.80	29.40	32.83	36.09
2	4.71	8.98	12.84	16.35	19.52	22.39	24.99	27.35	29.49
3	4.57	8.53	11.93	14.87	17.41	19.60	21.48	23.11	24.51
4	4.45	8.11	11.11	13.59	15.62	17.29	18.66	19.79	20.72
5	4.32	7.72	10.37	12.46	10.09	15.37	16.37	17.15	17.77
6	4.21	7.36	9.71	11.46	12.78	13.76	14.49	15.04	15.45
7	4.10	7.02	9.10	10.59	11.65	12.40	12.94	13.33	13.60
8	3.99	6.71	8.55	9.81	10.67	11.25	11.65	11.92	12.10
9	3.88	6.41	8.06	9.12	9.82	10.27	10.56	10.75	10.88

Table 10. Estimated Rates of Return

Estimated Rate of Return (%)	Years to Retirement							
	5	10	15	20	25	30	35	40
2	1.10	1.22	1.35	1.49	1.63	1.81	2.08	2.21
3	1.16	1.34	1.56	1.81	2.10	2.43	2.81	3.26
4	1.22	1.48	1.80	2.19	2.66	3.24	3.94	4.80
5	1.28	1.63	2.08	2.65	3.39	4.32	5.52	7.04
6	1.34	1.79	2.40	3.21	4.30	5.74	7.70	10.29

Table 11. Discount Rate

Discount Rate Factor (%)	Years to Retirement							
	5	10	15	20	25	30	35	40
2	.192	.091	.057	.041	.031	.024	.019	.016
3	.188	.087	.053	.037	.027	.021	.016	.013
4	.184	.083	.049	.033	.023	.017	.013	.010
5	.180	.079	.046	.030	.020	.015	.010	.008
6	.177	.075	.042	.027	.018	.012	.008	.006

WORKSHEET VIII: FILLING THE GAP:
TOTAL SAVINGS NEEDED

	Age Expected to Retire	Estimated Years in Retirement	Estimated Years to Retirement
Husband	_____	_____	_____
Wife	_____	_____	_____

Estimated Inflation Rate _____

Estimated Rate of Return _____

1. Desired Gross Annual Income   _____
   (Use 70 to 80% of present income)
   Husband _____
   Wife   _____

2. Estimated Annual Social Security Benefit
   (Amount you would receive if retiring this year)
   Husband _____
   Wife   _____   _____

3. Estimated Annual Income from Defined Benefit
   Plan(s) at Anticipated Retirement Date
   Husband 1 _____ 2 _____   _____
   Wife   1 _____ 2 _____   _____

4. Inflation Adjustment Factor—Table 8
   (Inflation Adjustment for Pension without COLA)
   Husband _____
   Wife   _____

5. Inflation Adjusted Pension Income
   (Line 3 times Line 4)
   Husband _____ × _____
   Wife   _____ × _____   _____

6. Annual Income from Social Security
   and Pension
   (Line 2 plus Line 5)   _____
   Husband _____
   Wife   _____

WORKSHEET VIII: FILLING THE GAP:
TOTAL SAVINGS NEEDED (cont.)

7. Additional Income Required
   (Line 1 minus Line 6)   _____
   Husband _____
   Wife   _____
8. Retirement Income Factor—Table 9
   (Estimated Years in Retirement and Inflation
   Factor)
   Husband _____
   Wife   _____
9. Savings Required at Retirement Date
   (Line 7 times Line 8)
   Husband _____ × _____
   Wife   _____ × _____   _____

WORKSHEET IX: FILLING THE GAP:
SAVINGS NEEDED PER YEAR

1. Amount Already Saved on Tax-Deferred Basis
   Include amounts in IRAs, profit-sharing plans,
   401(k)s, Keoghs, SEPs, cash value of life insurance.
   Husband _____
   Wife   _____

2. Value at Retirement (See Table 10: Estimated
   Rates of Return)
   (Estimated rate of return less inflation, based on
   years to retirement.)
   Husband _____ × _____ = _____
   Wife   _____ × _____ = _____   _____

3. Amounts Already Saved in Non-Tax-Deferred
   Investments
   Include amounts in savings, CDs, stocks, bonds,
   mutual funds, equity in rental real estate (not your
   principal residence).
   Husband _____
   Wife   _____
   Joint   _____

4. Value at Retirement (See Table 10: Estimated
   Rates of Return times Line 4)
   (Estimated rate of return less inflation and income
   taxes, based on years to retirement.)
   Husband _____ × _____ = _____
   Wife   _____ × _____ = _____
   Joint   _____ × _____ = _____   _____

5. Amount Still Needed for Retirement
   Line 9 on Worksheet VIII minus
   Line 3 and Line 5
   Husband _____
   Wife   _____   _____

WORKSHEET IX: FILLING THE GAP:
SAVINGS NEEDED PER YEAR (cont.)

6. See Table 11: Assumed Discount Rate
   (Estimated rate of return less inflation [and taxes if
   saving on after-tax basis], based on years to
   retirement.)
   Husband _____
   Wife   _____
7. Annual Savings Required for Retirement
   Line 6 times Line 5
   Husband _____ × _____ = _____
   Wife   _____ × _____ = _____   _____
8. Annual Employer Contribution to 401(k), Profit
   Sharing, ESOP, Etc.
   Husband _____
   Wife   _____   _____
9. Annual Savings Needed
   Line 7 minus Line 8
   Husband _____
   Wife   _____   _____

CHAPTER 9

Company and Other
Tax-Deferred Plans

The third leg of the retirement stool is the most important if you want to be financially independent before a pension and Social Security are available to you. This leg has to be solid and very sturdy if you expect to kiss the rat race good-bye by the time you are 45 or 50.

This leg involves everything you do all by yourself—*on your own*—to help give yourself financial independence. There are really two parts to this leg. The first, which I will discuss in this chapter, are the voluntary plans for savings your company may offer, wise use of your fringe benefits, and individual pension plans you can set up on your own. The second part is saving and investing with after-tax money. I'll discuss that in some detail in the next chapter.

Fortunately for everybody, both government and corporations have come to realize that most people will spend their money if they can get their hands on it, and will procrastinate almost forever on forming the habit of putting a set percentage of take-home pay right into the savings bank. So they—government and industry— have set up various so-called "voluntary tax-advantaged plans" to make saving not only easy and painless but automatic. Such plans channel automatic deductions from your paycheck into savings plans sponsored by the company. The deductions are "before taxes," so you pay no income tax on the deducted amount until you withdraw it from savings in your retirement years. The idea is "What you don't see, you don't spend."

Voluntary Plans Your Company May Offer

401(k) Plan.

This is probably the finest program available. It has become the most popular as companies change from defined benefit plans to defined contribution plans. Quite possibly your employer will match each contribution deducted from your paycheck with anywhere from 25 to 100 percent of your contribution up to a certain limit. A typical plan might say, "The company will match 50¢ for each $1 of the first 6 percent of pay. The employee contribution limit is 16 percent of pay."

> **EXAMPLE:**   If you make $50,000 and contribute 6 percent, you will have $4,500 credited to your account—$3,000 from your paycheck and $1,500 from your company. If you decide to increase your contribution to 10 percent—i.e., $5,000—the company's match will still be $1,500.

Neither the contributions nor the interest they earn are taxed until you begin withdrawals.

Contributions are stated as a percentage of your salary but the maximum amount you can contribute is limited to $8,728. The law allows an adjustment each year for inflation. Some details you should be aware of:

- While you pay no income taxes on the amount you contribute from your pay, and do not report it on your income-tax return, you do pay Social Security taxes on it. The annual tax-free limit of $8,728 applies only to the amount you elect to contribute. Your employer may make additional contributions but the total may not be more than either $30,000 or 25 percent of your total pay, whichever is less.
- If you participate in more than one plan, the limit applies to the total of all automatic deductions from all your paychecks and all contributions from all your employers.
- You are vested instantly for all contributions from your pay.

- The vesting of the contributions from your employer depends on how long you have been employed and on the vesting schedule. A certain percentage is added to your total vesting with each year until you are fully vested.
- If you change jobs, you may roll the amount in your 401(k) plan—the total amount in which you are vested—over to an Individual Retirement Account (IRA) or some other plan. (This can be a valuable benefit if you change jobs frequently or if, for instance, you decide not to work during the years when your children are very young.)
- Your employer cannot make contributions to a 401(k) plan unless you yourself make contributions.
- You should contribute at least as much as your employer will match. Even better, contribute the most the regulations allow. As noted earlier, if you don't see it, you won't spend it. Nothing can be more important than this basic rule.
- If you and your spouse are both working, be sure to join a 401(k) plan with the employer who provides the highest matching program. Even better, both of you join plans where you work.

Getting into a 401(k) plan is simple as pie: Just tell your paymaster or bookkeeper how much you want deducted from your pay, fill out an easy form, and you're in. The company takes care of administering the plan. You will usually be given a choice on the investment of your contributions. Investment options customarily include a fixed or guaranteed investment contract (GIC) fund, which invests with an insurance company. Other choices may include a balanced fund, which invests in both stocks and bonds to provide stability and growth, an equity fund for growth, or possibly company stock.

How will your 401(k) account grow? Assuming that you have 5 percent salary increases, and you make contributions of 6 percent of your pay (with your company adding 3 percent), and assuming your fund earns 8 percent interest (with interest credited quarterly

Table 12. 401(k) Plan Account Growth

Projected Account at the End of:	Current Salary	
	$35,000	$50,000
10 years	$ 56,748	$ 81,070
20 years	214,953	307,076
25 years	370,677	529,538

SOURCE: Hewitt Associates

on your contributions and at the end of the year on your company's matching funds), here is what to expect:

A BETTER INVESTMENT THAN A MERCEDES

Your 401(k) can be a gold mine if you just let it do its thing. Take it from Sandy, who was six years younger than her husband, George, when he retired at 51 from the telephone company. Sandy has a look-ahead mind. She not only had a "Honey do" list on the refrigerator every day for George (the note was always signed "Love, Sandy"), but 10 years earlier, when she was 35, Sandy had started putting 1 percent of her salary into her 401(k). She increased the contribution with each pay raise. After 10 years, her total stood at more than $70,000. "I only wish I had put in more at the beginning," says Sandy. "A 401(k) is a better investment than a Mercedes."

WHAT IF YOU NEED TO TAKE MONEY OUT OF A 401(K) PLAN WHILE YOU ARE STILL WORKING?

The regulations are stiff, but they do allow you to withdraw money from your plan before you are 59½ years old if you have to. (After you are 59½, any withdrawal is simply a matter of taking out the money and, unless you roll it over into some other "qualified" tax-deferred plan, paying taxes on it as ordinary income. And, of course, if you leave the company you can take out your money and pay the taxes and penalty or roll it over into an IRA without a penalty and taxes.)

To make a withdrawal before you are 59½, you must be faced with a financial hardship that is "immediate and heavy." What does that mean? The rules say your hardship is immediate and heavy if it is:

- for the purchase of a home
- for medical expenses for yourself, your spouse, or a dependent
- for college expenses for yourself, your spouse, or a child—but only for next year
- to prevent eviction or foreclosure on a mortgage.

You may make a withdrawal only if you have no other resources, including those of your spouse or your minor children, to meet the need. You are permitted to withdraw the funds in anticipation of the expense, before you have actually had to spend the money. Unless your withdrawal is to pay medical expenses that are more than 7.5 percent of your adjusted gross income, you will have to pay a penalty tax of 10 percent of the amount you take out. If it is for any of the other hardship purposes, you have to pay the penalty.

The most you may take out is the amount you yourself have contributed, plus its earnings. You are not allowed to take out any of the money your employer has put in. If you are considering a hardship withdrawal, it's best to check with your benefits administrator. NOTE: Your hardship withdrawal may not exceed the amount you need.

HOW ABOUT LOANS FROM 401(K) PLANS?

You can borrow from your plan. Probably 65 percent of the companies that offer 401(k) plans do make loans available. How do you qualify for a loan? Simply by having the money in the plan. You do not have to go through the application and approval process that a bank would put you through to get a loan. Your company establishes a rate of interest for 401(k) loans—usually tied to the prime rate (i.e., the base rate that large banks charge for corporate loans). The interest you pay then goes back into your own 401(k) plan, rather than to any lending institution. That's right—you pay yourself interest on your own loan.

There are a couple of limitations. You may not borrow more than 50 percent of the money in your plan—and not more than $50,000 no matter how much is in it. You must pay it back within five years unless it is a loan for a home, in which case your company sets the length of time—usually from 10 to 15 years. If you leave the company, whether you depart voluntarily or are let go, you must pay back the entire amount or it will be considered a taxable distribution. In that case, you will have to pay income tax on it, plus the 10 percent penalty if you are not yet 59½ years old.

All of this should encourage you to think long and hard before borrowing from your 401(k) plan. And remember—borrowing from your 401(k) is borrowing from your retirement.

403(b) Plan

If you work for a public school or another non-profit organization such as a hospital, government agency, or religious organization, this plan can give you tax-deferred savings just like the 401(k). The most you can put in each year is $9,500 or 25 percent of your salary, whichever is lower.

Company-sponsored Thrift Plan

This payroll-deduction plan is like the 401(k) except that your contribution is made with after-tax dollars. Your company may match (or partly match) your contributions. Usually you can make withdrawals without paying any penalty, if you are withdrawing only your own contributions, but you will have to pay a penalty if you withdraw money your company has put in. And you will probably have to pay tax on any interest the money in the account has earned.

Stock-Purchase Plan

Also like the 401(k) plan, this one uses your contributions, and those of your company (if any), to buy stock in the company for you. If it is a *stock-bonus plan*, you are allowed to buy the stock with after-tax dollars. Some companies permit employees to buy company stock at a discount as much as 15 percent below the current market price. The Internal Revenue Service says, however, that the discounted amount must be treated as compensation, so you have to pay income tax on it. WARNING! Company loyalty is praiseworthy and commendable—but think hard before you put your entire nest egg into shares in your company. It is your hard-earned money—no one else's.

Andy's Stock In His Company.   In addition to his profit-sharing plan, Andy has been buying stock in his company ever since he started there 23 years ago. Its value will add another $100,000 to his half million from the profit sharing. Andy calls it "my painless purchase—paycheck by paycheck," as payroll deductions have kept the plan moving.

Checking Out Your Fringe Benefits

Most employers, unless they are extremely small businesses, provide "fringe benefits" that range from medical insurance to tuition reimbursement. These are the "extras," over and above your salary, that often help to make one job or employer more attractive than another. They can make a big difference in your budget and in your attitude toward the company. The better the fringe benefits, the more likely it is that you will want to stay with the company and not change jobs. At some companies, however, an increase in pay may be offset by a reduction in fringe benefits. And, among corporate executives, a top-notch fringe benefit package may be worth as much as hundreds of thousands of dollars more in compensation, over the long haul.

Once you gain a thorough understanding of your company's benefit "package," you can fit the available benefits to your individual needs. If you and your spouse are both employed, but by different companies, you may find different benefit plans available. Some companies provide flexible packages—sometimes called "cafeteria plans"—from which you can pick and choose the benefits you want. You and your spouse can coordinate each other's plans so you don't duplicate coverage and so you get the lowest cost on each benefit.

Medical and Dental Insurance

Probably no fringe benefit is more valuable or important to you than medical and dental insurance. What is offered varies greatly from company to company, with some providing medical policies but no dental policies, some paying premiums in full for their employees, others making partial payments. Even if your company insists that you pay the entire premium yourself, you have an advantage because you are in a group. An individual policy would cost substantially more. The fact is that in recent years employers have asked their employees to pay more and more of the group insurance premiums because the costs of such insurance have been skyrocketing. You can understand why: The surgical techniques that have become commonplace—open heart, laser breakup of cataracts, laparoscopy, to name only a few—are as expensive as they are sophisticated. The cost of a day or two in the hospital has zoomed, too. And your doctor (whose *own* liability insurance has gone through the ceiling!) is charging you more than you ever dreamed of paying for an office visit. The insurance companies raise their rates to cover the costs, and your company asks you to help pay the higher rates. In addition, many companies have also been cutting back severely on the amount of reimbursement (i.e., the percentage of the total claim) for medical costs that the insurance provides.

Another hidden reason why employers are cutting back is a new accounting requirement that says employers must identify the costs of future medical benefits as a liability on their balance sheets.

Some employers give you no choice about what insurance company provides your major medical policy. Others let you choose among several. If you are shopping, it won't hurt to do some checking and comparisons:

- How does the deductible work? Per person, or per family? If it is per person, multiply it by the number of people covered.
- Do you pay off the deductible at the start of each new year, or does it apply to each claim—no matter how many claims you file?
- Can you apply any expense toward paying the deductible? What is the stop-loss limit? Most companies pay 80 percent of your claims each year (once you have gone past the deductible amount) until you reach $2,000; above that, they pay 100 percent. That is called the stop-loss limit.
- Above that, what is the absolute top limit the company will pay?
- Also after you have paid the deductible, what percentage of each claim (i.e., coinsurance) do you have to pay? Is it the typical 20 percent?
- Are there any other limitations?

TIP: If you are young and healthy, and so is your spouse, consider increasing the deductible on your family major medical policy, so you pay for more of the routine medical costs and the insurance company can cut down its share of the risk. And tell them to set the stop-loss limit higher than is customary. These two steps (or either of them) should help to reduce the cost of your major medical insurance.

If your company is like most, it may provide more than one health insurance plan, ranging from policies offered by the private insurance companies to the Blue Cross/Blue Shield in your state to Health Maintenance Organizations (HMOs). They all have different rules on deductibles (i.e., how much they deduct from a medical bill or claim you present, before they pay it). Most folks simply look at the deductible before deciding which company to go with.

But you should look at more than that. Think of the total out-of-pocket expense you are taking on, including the premium, the deductible, and copayments (i.e, where you and your spouse are covered at your respective places of work).

The key thing is not to overinsure yourself and your family. Carefully review your medical expenses over the last few years. Figure out what you would have actually paid *under each of the options you are considering*. Then decide. If, for instance, you are a healthy young person, be willing to accept a high deductible in order to lower the cost of your premium. You will still be covered for any major illness, since the policy will pay for all covered expenses above your out-of-pocket maximum for any one year.

If you have a growing family, or anticipate some major medical problems, you may opt for a plan with a lower deductible or for an HMO, which pays 100 percent of medical expenses. In either case, you will probably find that the premium cost is higher than for a policy with a high deductible.

If you and your spouse are both employed and health coverage is provided to each of you, do your homework on which company provides which services. If the company pays for the coverage or the cost is minimal at both employers, you will probably not want to drop either one. But if each of you is paying the premium cost at your place of work, you will be smart to consolidate your coverage under one plan.

It is even possible that, if you both have coverage, you can submit claims to both insurance companies and recover as much as 100 percent of your medical expenses (e.g., if one plan—the primary plan—pays for 80 percent of a medical claim, the other—the secondary plan—pays for the additional 20 percent copayment). WARNING: Check this out carefully—many companies, determined to get control of soaring insurance costs—are eliminating coordination of medical benefits.

Duplicate coverage of spouses who work for separate companies is common in health insurance, so probably three-quarters of companies offer flexible plans that allow an employee to opt out of medical coverage. Think and check carefully before you do that.

Review your plan and your spouse's, because limits vary from plan to plan. How well would you be covered if a catastrophe occurred?

Such plans are usually called "cafeteria plans" or "flex plans." They have developed as the number of two-income families, with both spouses working full-time, has grown phenomenally during the 1980s. They let you pick and choose certain benefits. How does it work? You each get an "allotment of credits," which is really a fixed amount of money, at your company. From a menu of benefits offered—medical, dental, life, and disability insurance—you select those you want. Within each, you will probably find several levels of coverage. If what you select costs more than the allotment, you pay the difference from your paycheck. If it costs less, the company will probably give you several choices: Take the money in cash, put it into a savings account, or even "buy" some additional vacation time.

TIP: If you are giving up medical coverage because you're using your spouse's plan, make sure your employer will permit you to sign up again if circumstances change. What if your spouse, who now has the medical plan, retires early, loses the coverage, and wants to be covered by the plan where you work—but you yourself are covered only by your spouse's plan? Will your company keep that door open for you? And what if a divorce should occur? You might have to reenroll in your own company's plan.

Then, too, you must remember that preexisting conditions are usually not covered by an insurance company until at least a year has passed. Maternity benefits usually do not become available until the end of the first year of coverage.

If your company offers a cash reward for not taking advantage of the insurance they offer, hoping you will get your coverage at your spouse's workplace, think very carefully before you "buy out" of your company's health plan. Don't kid yourself into taking the extra cash and spending it, or latching onto those enticing extra vacation days, tempting as all that may be when you are in good health. You never know when an accident or a major illness will change things. Seriously consider asking your employer to put the money into a 401(k) plan—after all, you are working toward voluntary early retirement.

Not every company that offers a medical plan includes a dental plan. Consider yourself lucky if your company does. Probably it will not pay for routine checkups and tooth cleaning, and quite likely it will pay less than the standard fees charged by most dentists for bridges, crowns, and orthodontic work. Still, you're lucky to get it. NOTE: Oral surgery and some periodontal work are considered surgery, so they are paid for by your medical insurance—even if you don't have dental coverage.

Getting and maintaining sound health insurance demands plenty of careful thinking and planning. Some good questions to ask:

- How much do I myself have to pay, regardless of what the company provides?
- How about my dependents—do I pay for them, or are they all (spouse, children) included in the basic coverage?
- What is the deductible on both medical and dental claims?
- Is there any limit on how many claims we can make in a year—or their dollar amounts?
- Which illnesses or procedures (e.g., psychotherapy, psychiatric treatment, routine annual checkups, chiropractic treatment, chronic allergy, routine eye examinations) are not covered?

Reimbursement Account or Flexible Spending Account (FSA)

This is an idea that is relatively new. It is growing rapidly. Your company withholds a certain amount from your paycheck *before taxes* (i.e., exempt from federal income tax, Social Security tax, state taxes in all states except New Jersey and Pennsylvania, and the 1.45 percent Medicare payroll tax). You then use money from your FSA account to pay for child care, if you need to, and for the health-care expenses that your major medical and dental plans do not reimburse you for, such as "well baby" checkups at the pediatrician's, drug and alcohol treatments, hair transplants, remedial reading for a dyslexic child, routine eye examinations and glasses (even nonprescription sunglasses), annual physicals, and nonprescription "over the counter" medications.

How does it work? You check your budget and your experience over the past couple of years, and tell your company how much you want to set aside for the coming year. Do your homework carefully, noting how much you yourself paid last year in deductibles the insurance company took off your medical and dental claims for coinsurance, and what you paid for the many services that the insurance company does not cover, such as routine checkups, eyeglasses, preventive care.

CAUTION: The government says that any money left in your FSA at the end of the year must be given back to your company, so do your figuring precisely and conservatively. Some of the facts you should know about:

- Your FSA money can be used to pay for a Health-Care Reimbursement Account or a Dependent Day-Care Reimbursement Account—or both.
- Your employer sets a limit on the amount you may put into your Health-Care Account; most companies impose a limit anywhere from $1,500 to $2,500.
- While only 2 percent of the top one thousand American corporations are offering FASs, many small businesses provide them.
- By law, the limit on a Dependent Day-Care Account is $5,000 a year, if you file a joint tax return.
- Your child covered by a Dependent Day-Care Account must be younger than 13.

- If you are a taxpayer in the 28 percent bracket (i.e., with a taxable income of $34,000 to $82,150 on your joint return), paying $5,000 in day-care costs from an FSA will save you about $1,400 in federal income taxes. If you are in the 31 percent bracket, the saving will be about $1,550.
- If yours is a two-income family, you may gain more if your FSA account is funded by the spouse who earns the lower of the two salaries, because the Social Security tax is levied only on wages up to a certain amount; since the FSA is exempt from Social Security tax, let the one who may not earn as much as the Social Security limit in the entire year be the one who gains the exemption. (If the higher-earning spouse pays for the FSA, and earns more than the maximum for Social Security withholding, it will come off the top, where the exemption won't do any good.)
- Be sure to pay attention to your FSA in the fall of the year. That's when your company will hold an "enrollment period." You must then decide how much to put into your next year's FSA through payroll deductions, or settle for the same amount as this year—or perhaps be locked out entirely if you do not renew.
- Before the last day of the year, spend any unspent balance in your account—buy over-the-counter medicines, new glasses, whatever is eligible. Otherwise, under the law, the company keeps your leftover balance.

Speaking of the end of the year, that's a good time to review the amount of your 401(k) contribution. Are you having the maximum payroll deduction that is permitted before taxes? Can you add some after-tax money, too, to help build your early retirement nest egg? How about the investment of your 401(k) savings? Should any be changed? Your company will allow you to make changes more frequently, but year-end is a good time to sit down and really look things over.

Your goal, of course, is to get the most you can out of the benefits

Table 13. Adding Up the Tax Savings

	Salary		
	$75,000	*$95,000*	*$130,000*
Fringe Benefits	*Amounts Contributed*		
401(k)—6% of Salary	$ 4,500	$ 5,700	$ 7,800
Health-Care Account	2,000	2,000	2,000
Dependent-Care Account	5,000	5,000	5,000
Total	$11,500	$12,700	$14,900
Tax Savings			
401(k)	$1,422	$1,801	$2,687
Health-Care Account	632	632	689
Dependent-Care Account	1,580	1,580	1,722
Total Tax Savings	$3,634	$4,013	$5,098

Assumptions:
State Tax Rate—5%
Federal Tax Rate—28% for $75,000 and $95,000;
     31% for $130,000

SOURCE: The Wyatt Company

your company offers. Careful review can not only mean paying lower taxes but adding significantly to your retirement savings.

How do the savings add up? If you take advantage of some of the fringe benefits at work, such as a 401(k) and a Flexible Spending Account (if it is offered), you can save a substantial amount in federal income taxes. Let's assume that you are a two-income family, with a combined income of $95,000. Each of you puts 6 percent of your pay into a 401(k) plan. With your Flexible Spending Account, you are putting $5,000 into dependent day-care and $2,000 into health care. The tax savings add up to $4,013. If your combined incomes are $130,000, the tax saving is $5,098. Not bad. Tax savings are helping you pay for child care and medical expenses, and at the same time you are saving for retirement.

Life Insurance

The fringe benefits at most companies include life insurance. Coverage is typically from one to two times your annual pay, and usually you may buy additional coverage at the low group rate, with the premium deducted from your paycheck. Before you sign up for this, however, compare the rates with term insurance you can buy on your own.

When you leave your company, you will be invited to convert from the group policy to an individual policy. This can be expensive. But think ahead. Since you are planning early retirement, you may be wise to buy more insurance now, when you are young and healthy and rates (which are based on your age when you buy the policy) are lower.

Disability Insurance

This is another fringe benefit that is offered by some companies, not by others. Check carefully and, if your company (or your spouse's) does not offer it, buy a policy on your own. Disability has a way of sneaking up on you when you are not looking. A single accident can put you out of commission for several weeks or even months—long enough to outlive your company's interest in printing out your regular paycheck. If at that point there is no insurance coverage, you will find yourself wiser but sadder.

Health Care After You Retire

When you retire early, the cost of health care is one of your most pressing concerns. Traditionally, most companies that provide health care as a fringe benefit have continued it for retirees, but today more and more companies, looking hard at the cost, are reducing or ending such coverage. That trend is not about to change.

Today, many companies want you to complete 10 years of service before they declare you qualified for full benefits. Others limit you to a specific dollar amount of claims each year. Since no federal law requires any company to fund health benefits for retirees, your company can make its own rules.

Suppose you are offered an early retirement package and health insurance is not part of the deal. Try to negotiate for it. If you are over 55, your company may be willing to keep you covered until you reach 65, when Medicare kicks in. Make sure you get a firm understanding of the terms, and get it in writing—most plans can be changed at the discretion of the company.

If you are moving ahead on your plan to retire early, there is a way to buy health insurance through your employer. You take advantage of the Consolidated Omnibus Budget Reconciliation Act of 1985—known as COBRA. If your company has a health insurance plan, it requires it to offer continuing coverage to employees, their spouses and dependent children who otherwise lose coverage if you terminate employment, or if the company terminates your employment for reasons other than misconduct or reduces your hours of employment.

COBRA coverage continues for 18 months (or for 29 months if you are disabled). It covers your beneficiaries—surviving spouse and dependent children—for 36 months if you should die or if a divorce or legal separation should occur. The coverage must be identical to that you had while you were employed. The only catch: You must pay 102 percent of the premium, and you pay it directly to your former employer.

At the end of the coverage period, your former employer must offer you conversion to an individual policy if the group policy includes the conversion privilege (as it is required to do in most states). Chances are you will not find the coverage in the individual policy as generous as in the group plan. *And* it will be more expensive.

If your spouse is still working when you take your early retirement, of course, you may make out much better by getting your health benefits through his or her plan.

Health Care When You Work for Yourself

What if you are self-employed or become self-employed? How can you get health insurance at a rate lower than the expensive individual policies you've heard about? Do some research before you go to an insurance agent. See if you qualify for membership in an "affinity group." For instance, can you join the local Chamber of Commerce? Many chambers offer medical plans to their members. If you are a lawyer, check with the bar association for a group plan. In fact, many of the professional associations provide group insurance for their members.

Individual Pension Plans

Three different pension plans that you can set up on your own are worth knowing about: IRAs, Keoghs, and SEPs.

1. Individual Retirement Account: IRA

The IRA has a checkered past. Until 1982, you could set one up only if there was no pension or profit-sharing plan where you worked. Then, to stimulate individual savings, the law changed to allow anyone who had earned income to contribute to an IRA and deduct the amount from federal income taxes. But 1987 brought another change in the rules. The maximum you can contribute and claim as a tax deduction is limited to $2,000, or $2,250 if you are a one-income family or $4,000 if both spouses are working. And all of the earnings of the IRA (i.e., the interest the financial institution pays on the deposit) are not taxable until you take the money out of the account.

Today the rules have a big "it depends . . ." in front of them. The deductibility of your IRA contribution depends on the level of your income and on your membership in a qualified pension plan. Here's how it works:

• If you or your spouse are not covered by any pension plan, you may make an IRA contribution that is fully tax-deductible— regardless of your income.

Table 14. IRA Deductibility

(*If You Are In An Employer-Sponsored Plan*)			
If You Are:	*If Your Adjusted Gross Income Is:*		
Single	$25,000 Or Less	Between $25,000 & $35,000	$35,000 Or More
Married Filing Jointly	$40,000 Or Less	Between $40,000 & $50,000	$50,000 Or More
Married Filing Singly	Not Applicable	Under $10,000	$10,000 Or More
Your IRA Contribution	Fully Deductible	Partially Deductible	Not Deductible

• If your adjusted gross income on a joint return is $40,000 or less (or $25,000 or less if you are single), you may deduct the full amount of your IRA contribution even if you are covered by a qualified pension plan. If you are self-employed and have set up a Keogh plan, you are considered a member of such a plan.

• If your adjusted gross income on a joint return is between $40,000 and $50,000 (or between $25,000 and $35,000 on a single return), that maximum tax-free contribution of $2,000 (or $2,500 for a one-income family or $4,000 for a two-income family) will come down—in steps—by $200 for each additional $1,000 of income.

• If your joint return is higher than $50,000 in adjusted gross income, or your single return is higher than $35,000, you can forget the tax deduction—you don't get it.

• If either you or your spouse is not working, your working spouse may contribute to an IRA established in your name. The total amount you are allowed to put into *both* accounts each year is $2,250, or 100 percent of the pay of the working spouse—whichever is less. Can you divide that $2,250 into the two accounts any way you choose? Yes, as long as no more than $2,000 goes into either one. NOTE: The individual whose name is on the account has control of the account. And if a divorce should occur, a former spouse who gets alimony but has no earned income is allowed to use alimony money to continue the contributions to his or her IRA, up to the $2,000 annual limit.

• Even if you are not eligible to take the income-tax deduction, you may make contributions up to $2,000 to your IRA and the *earnings* (i.e., the interest the financial institution pays) will not be taxed until you take the money out. In addition, when you do withdraw the money you once put in, you will not have to pay income tax on it—it was after-tax dollars when you salted it away.

RECORD-KEEPING NOTE: Always keep tax-deductible and non-tax-deductible accounts separate. The rule to remember is that when you withdraw your tax-deductible contributions some day, you will have to pay income taxes on them *and* on the interest they have earned, but when you withdraw your non-tax-deductible contributions you will have to pay income taxes only on the interest earned.

If you are making non-tax-deductible contributions to an IRA, you must file Form 8606 with your income-tax return. The form makes you show the amount of non-tax-deductible contributions made during the year as well as the value of all your IRAs as of the end of the year.

If you're like most folks, you may have more than one IRA in more than one bank or other financial institution. Good record keeping is important. It means you can tell instantly when a CD is to mature, so you are primed to reinvest the funds, as well as what yields you are receiving and whether the IRA contribution was tax-deductible or not.

There is no law saying you have to put away the maximum $2,000 (or $2,250 or $4,000) each year. You may put in as much or as little as you want, and you may do it in a single deposit or monthly or quarterly—whatever suits you best. The amount may vary from

Table 15. How Much Can an IRA Add Up To?

| | Amount of Annual Contribution | | | | | |
| | $500 | | $1,000 | | $2,000 | |
Starting at Age	At Age 50	At Age 59½	At Age 50	At Age 59½	At Age 50	At Age 59½
25	$39,477	$82,071	$78,954	$164,143	$157,909	$328,287
35	14,662	30,482	29,324	60,964	58,649	121,929
40	7,823	16,264	15,645	32,525	31,291	65,053

one deposit to the next. You may even skip one or more years if you have to.

But keep in mind that timing—the moment when you make your IRA contribution—does make a difference. Many, many people wait until they are filing their tax returns on the April 15 deadline the year after the tax year—for that is the deadline for opening an IRA, or contributing to one, for the preceding year. They have wasted precious interest-earning time. When you make an IRA deposit, it starts earning tax-deferred interest immediately, so a contribution made in January gains 15 months of tax-deferred interest over a contribution made when you file your tax return in April of the following year.

How much can an IRA add up to, by the time you reach the age of 59½? Let's take a look. Assuming that you start now and make annual contributions until you are 50, that they earn 8 percent interest, compounded annually, and that you leave them on deposit until you are 59½, check table 15 to see where you will come out at age 50 and at 59½. If you need the funds before you reach 59½, you will have to pay a 10 percent penalty, plus income tax on the amount you take out (the same rules apply to 401(k) withdrawals, rollover IRAs, and any other tax-advantaged retirement accounts). But it will probably still work to your advantage to make contributions to an IRA, even if you take out the money before you are 59½, because the penalty and tax might be offset by the rate of interest and the growth you have gained over a certain period. Before you decide *not* to invest in an IRA read the section on early withdrawals on page 135.

Of course, if you are retiring to something else—say, another career—and have earned income, you may continue annual contributions to your IRA.

How about *IRA rollovers*? You may move IRA money to another bank or investment form by direct transfer or by rolling it over. In a direct transfer, the money is moved from one institution to another by direct order; you never get your hands on it. In a rollover, you receive a check for the amount of money and must then deposit it within 60 days in another IRA account. If you do not complete the rollover within 60 days, you must pay taxes on the full amount and, if you are under age 59½, you must pay a 10 percent penalty. (The same rules apply if you receive a lump-sum payout from a corporate pension plan.) WARNING: You are permitted only one rollover per year.

You have plenty of choices about where to put your IRA money. Banks, insurance companies, mutual funds, and brokerage firms offer IRA accounts—but you cannot go so far as to invest IRA savings in collectibles (e.g., art objects, antiques, stamps). Most people decide on a particular savings account, put their IRA money in it, and leave it there—but you are allowed to spread it to more than one type of account if you wish, provided you don't exceed the limits on total contributions. You have to look at your own situation and make a decision. (NOTE: Investment alternatives are discussed in chapter 10 on saving and investing.)

The distributions rules are pretty much the same, whether your account is an IRA, a self-employed plan (Keogh), or a pre-tax savings plan. See section later in this chapter for details.

2. Keogh Plan

If you are either fully or partly self-employed, this is the retirement savings plan for you. You may, however, also contribute to an IRA. Since the Keogh is considered a qualified plan, the percentage of your IRA contribution that is tax-deductible will depend on the size of your income.

As with IRAs, the rules on Keoghs have changed over recent years. Originally they were subject to limitations and benefits that were tighter than those of corporate retirement plans. As a self-employed individual, you were limited to contributing a maximum of $2,500 a year. This rule caused many self-employed people to incorporate so they could gain better tax benefits for their retirement savings. In 1974, the rule changed, allowing you to put as much as 15 percent of earned income or $7,500, whichever was lower, into your Keogh plan. Then in 1982 Congress established parity between Keoghs and corporate pension plans, making the maximum limits for both a defined benefit and a defined contribution the same as those for corporate plans.

Despite these incentives, not many people who are self-employed and who are not incorporated have participated. In 1987, only 5.6 percent of some 10 million unincorporated self-employed people contributed to Keogh plans.

Today you may put up to 25 percent of your net self-employed income or $30,000, whichever is less, into your Keogh plan. That contribution, based on "net earned income," is deductible from your taxable income. Your "net earned income" is your net profit, as shown on Schedule C of your federal income tax return, less the amount you are contributing to the retirement plan. This means that your *effective* annual contribution is actually less than 25 percent—20 percent if you have a money-purchase plan, or 13.04 percent if you have a profit-sharing plan.

You must open your Keogh account by December 31 of the current year (no postponing until April 15!). But you are allowed to keep that opening deposit small, using it to establish your claim for the deduction for the year's entire contribution, and later add more (by the date when you file your tax return) when you have worked out Schedule C and know where you stand.

The earnings you put into your Keogh plan grow tax deferred until you start withdrawals.

Say you have a couple of employees who are at least 21 years old and have worked for you for two years. You must cover them as well. Contributions you make on their behalf are tax deductible as a business expense. It's a good idea to check with your accountant if you have employees. And be ready for the fact that the paperwork for a Keogh plan is more complicated than for an IRA.

The rules on how you invest your Keogh money and how you take distributions are much like those for the other plans.

3. Simplified Employee Pension (SEP)

Some small businesses offer retirement plans, but many are reluctant to establish them because administering them, including compliance with all the federal regulations, is such a headache. A SEP makes it a lot easier; it keeps record keeping, paperwork, and reporting to a minimum.

What happens is that your small-business employer establishes an Individual Retirement Account (IRA) for each eligible employee. The rules say that you, as an employee, must be immediately vested in whatever contribution your employer makes, and you usually direct the investment of the funds. SEPs may be set up by corporations, unincorporated businesses, partnerships, or self-employed individuals.

How much can be put into your SEP? The maximum each year, both from your employer and from deductions from your pay, is 15 percent of your pay or $30,000, whichever is less. The option of taking payroll deductions to put money into a SEP is available only to those who work in firms that have 25 or fewer employees—*and* at least 50 percent of them must elect to contribute to the SEP.

How much can you put in tax free? Up to $8,728 a year. This limit is indexed each year for inflation. While the amount that you put into a SEP is not included as wages on your W-2 form, it is subject to the Social Security tax. Neither your contributions nor the earnings of the account are taxed until you withdraw them. The handling of distributions is like that for other qualified retirement plans.

Your employer is not *required* to make any contribution. If the company is having a bad year, contributions may be cut back or eliminated. But if contributions are being made, the following regulations apply.

- Your employer must make contributions for all employees who have reached 21 years of age and have worked for the employer for the last three out of five years.
- To be eligible, you must have been paid at least $355 during the year.
- If you work part-time, you must meet the three-out-of-five rule.
- Even if you worked for only a short period during the year— but worked enough to earn the $355 minimum—your employer *must* make a contribution.
- If (heaven forbid!) you die during the year, your employer *must* make a contribution—which will, of course, go into your estate.

Even though SEP is available, very few small businesses provide any retirement plan for employees. Why wouldn't your small-business employer want to provide an SEP? One reason is that, because you are vested immediately in the contribution your employer puts in, he or she is afraid you won't stay with the company for a long period—that you'll "take the money and run." That takes away funds that your employer would like to use to reward those who stay with the business for a long time.

4. Salary Reduction Simplified Employee Pension (SARSEP)

This is a hybrid—a cross between an IRA and a 401(k) plan. It is for companies that have fewer than 25 employees, with at least 50 percent of them participating. Both you, as an employee, and your employer are allowed to contribute, but your employer is not required to do so.

Your annual contribution to a SARSEP can be as much as to a 401(k)—either $8,728 or up to 15 percent of your pay, whichever is less. It is before-tax money, so you gain that benefit. If your employer wishes to, he or she may contribute any amount up to 15 percent of your salary, but the total of employer contributions and your own deductions from payroll may not be more than 25 percent of your pay or $30,000.

The IRA rules about early withdrawals and paying taxes at the time when you take distribution apply to a SARSEP.

"But How Do I Get My Money Out of a Retirement Plan?"

The bureaucratic word for it is "distribution"—when you take money out, it is "distributed" even though it goes only to you and despite the dictionary definition ("to divide among several or many"). Come to think of it, it does also go partly to the government as a tax, so there may be a little logic to the word.

All plans, whether IRA (including rollover IRAs), Keogh, corporate, or SEP, have very specific rules and regulations about distribution.

Early Withdrawal

If you take any of your money out of one of these plans before you turn 59½, you must pay a penalty. The only exceptions are (1) if you are permanently disabled, or (2) if the distribution is part of a series of substantially equal payments over the rest of your life or over the joint lives of a beneficiary and you. NOTE: Early withdrawal from 401(k) plans because of financial hardship was discussed on page 113. If you have died, however, your beneficiary is not subject to the penalty for early distribution.

What is the penalty? It is 10 percent of the amount you take out of the plan, and, for tax purposes, you must treat the withdrawal as ordinary income.

EXAMPLE: Suppose you withdraw $5,000 from your IRA. You must add $5,000 to your taxable income. If you are in the 28 percent tax bracket, this will mean a tax of $1,400 (i.e., 28 percent of $5,000). In addition, you must pay the penalty of 10 percent of $5,000, or $500. The total tax, then, is $1,900, leaving you with a net distribution of $3,100.

If at age 25 you had started making annual contributions of $2,000 to an IRA, the value at age 50 would be $157,909.

If you had put the same amount into a taxable investment, assuming you are in the 28 percent tax bracket, the value at age 50 would be $112,202.

What would happen if you took early withdrawals starting when you are 50 and paid the penalty and the tax? Suppose you take out 10 percent at the beginning of each year, pay the 10 percent penalty and the taxes, and leave the rest on deposit at an 8 percent rate of return (assuming that you are in the 28 percent tax bracket and the IRA contributions were tax deductible). Table 16 shows the beginning and ending balances for the next 10 years.

How would this compare with making withdrawals from your taxable fund of $112,202 if you took out the same net amount (the withdrawal less penalty and taxes)? At the end of the same period,

Table 16. IRA Early Withdrawals

Age	Beginning Balance	10% Withdrawal	Withdrawal Net of Tax and Penalty	Interest 8%	Ending Balance
50	$157,909	$15,791	$9,790	$11,369	$153,487
51	153,487	15,349	9,516	11,051	149,189
52	149,189	14,919	9,250	10,742	145,012
53	145,012	14,501	8,991	10,441	140,952
54	140,952	14,095	8,739	10,149	137,006
55	137,006	13,701	8,495	9,864	133,169
56	133,169	13,317	8,257	9,588	129,440
57	129,440	12,944	8,025	9,320	125,816
58	125,816	12,582	7,801	9,059	122,293
59	122,293	12,229	7,582	8,805	118,869

you would have a balance of $75,721. Remember, you started with $45,707 more in the IRA account, and the balance kept growing on a tax-deferred basis, while taxes had to be paid on the interest earned on your non-IRA account. The break-even point between an IRA and a taxable account depends on your tax bracket and your rate of return. Suppose your bracket is 28 percent and you are getting a return of 8 percent. The break-even point will be about 11 years. That means that after about 11 years it will have been worth putting the money into an IRA, taking it out, and paying the penalty and taxes. Any time before 11 years, it is not worth it. Of course, if you can get a higher rate of return on your money, the break-even point will be earlier.

If your IRA contributions are nondeductible, the tax on early withdrawals will apply only to the interest or gains that you have earned—not to the money you have put in yourself from your after-tax dollars. The penalty, nevertheless, still applies.

How Can You Avoid the Penalty?

You can avoid the penalty. If you are retiring early, or have been offered an incentive program that encourages you to retire early, the early withdrawal will be important. The way to avoid the penalties is to take distribution in a series of equal and regular payments made (at least annually) over your lifetime or the joint lifetimes of a beneficiary and you. How much can you take? IRS tables determine the amount.

The rules include these points:

- You must continue the withdrawals for at least five years or until you reach 59½, whichever comes later.
- If you change your mind between the time when you start taking payments and the time when you turn 59½, and if you are not disabled, you must pay a penalty in the year when you make the change.
- If you change the method of distribution after you have reached 59½, and if you are neither disabled nor have received substan-

tially equal payments for at least five years, you must pay a penalty. Not only will you pay a penalty but you will "play catch-up" with Uncle Sam. You will have to pay the taxes and the late-payment interest on those taxes for each year in which you took a distribution.

Thus if you retire at the age of 52 and roll your pension money over into an IRA, you may begin withdrawals immediately without penalty—as long as you get equal payments until you reach 59½.

EXAMPLE

John Smith, who is 52, decides to start taking annuity-type withdrawals. At 58, he makes a new decision: He wants to take the balance in a lump sum. He must pay a 10 percent penalty on both the lump sum and on all the payments he has had since he was 52, plus taxes and interest, because he is not yet 59½ and he is changing his method of distribution. Note that he has, however, received equal payments for the required five years.

Suppose you are 57 when you start taking withdrawals. You must take them until you are 62 (i.e., for five years).

EXAMPLE

Mary Jones starts taking payments at 57, but decides when she is 61 that she wants to change the amount of her payout. Because her arrangement was not in force for the five-year minimum, she must pay a penalty and taxes and interest on those payments she took between the ages of 57 and 61. She will not have to pay a penalty on payments under her new arrangement, because she is older than 59½.

How Much Can You Take Out in Equal Payments?

The IRS sets the rules for taking early withdrawals without any penalty. The most common method uses the insurance company's current annuity purchase rate. You take the number of thousands of dollars in the fund balance and multiply that by the current annuity purchase rate times 12 to arrive at the amount that must be taken out annually for the next five years or until you reach 59½, *whichever comes later.*

Use the same beginning balance of $157,909 as shown in table 16. A 50-year-old male would use the *current* annuity purchase rate of $7.27 per $1,000 in the account. The annual withdrawal would be $13,776 per year ($7.27 multiplied by 157.91 multiplied by 12). Taxed as ordinary income (at 28 percent rate) the net amount you would receive would be $9,918. Remember, if you start at age 50, you must receive payments until you are at least 59½. If you wait until age 55 when the multiplier is $7.70, your annual withdrawal (before taxes) will be $14,591 and you must take equal payments until you are at least 60 in order to satisfy the five-year rule. The multiplier for women is less than for men—a woman at age 50 would receive $13,018 and at age 55 the annual withdrawal would be $13,662. The important thing to remember is that you *cannot* make discretionary withdrawals—they must be a fixed amount.

The balance in the account continues to grow on a tax-deferred basis. When you have satisfied the legal requirements you can leave the balance in the account until you are 70½ or take the balance and pay the taxes on it.

According to a private letter ruling (PLR) by the IRS, a request for this type of distribution should be in writing and the following endorsement should be added: "The election shall be irrevocable until the later of five years following the first payment or the owner attaining age 59½. Until then, the owner may not partially or totally surrender the policy, assign it or use it as security for a debt, or change the duration or method of determining payments. Payments will be made on an annual, semi-annual, quarterly, or monthly basis as agreed to by the company and the owner."

WARNING: Talk with your accountant or financial planner before you decide to take early withdrawals from an IRA, 401(k), or any other tax-deferred investment. Don't do this two days before your planned independence day. Sit down with such a financial adviser a year or more ahead and look at all possible alternatives. Remember that your situation is unique. No one else's is quite like it.

EXTRA WARNING: Be careful about taking *excess distributions*. You may be penalized if you withdraw more than the limits prescribed by the Feds from either an employer retirement plan or an IRA. Those limits are $750,000 for a lump sum qualifying for income averaging, and $150,000 for all other IRA distributions. The penalty is 15 percent of the amount that is in excess of the limit. Is any type of distribution exempt from this excess penalty? Yes. If you are rolling over a distribution from a qualified plan into an IRA, it is exempt.

Distributions

Take a moment to look far ahead. Between the ages of 59½ and 70½, how much you take out of your IRA or other savings plan is up to you. You may take distributions in any amount you wish, or leave the money to grow on a tax-deferred basis until you are 70½. But once you reach 70½, you have no choice: You must start taking distributions. The deadline for starting is April 1 of the calendar year that follows the calendar year in which you reach that age. And here comes a trap: If you wait until the year that follows the year when you turn 70½, you will have to take your first distribution before April 1 and then take a second distribution before December 31. This could substantially increase your taxable income. So the word to the wise is this: Take your first distribution in Year A (i.e., the calendar year during which you turn 70½) even though you are allowed to delay until April 1 of Year B, or else you will have to take two distributions in Year B. Each year after that, you must take a distribution by December 31.

How much do you take? You will want to take out as little as possible, to make the money last as long as possible. The rules set a required minimum that is fixed by the amount you have in the account and the life expectancy of a person your age. The IRS

Table 17. IRA Withdrawal Table

Present Age	Anticipated Life Expectancy (Years)		Approximate % of Accum. Funds That Must Be Taken Out Each Year*	
	Male	Female	Male	Female
70	12.1	15.0	8.33%	6.66%
71	11.6	14.4	8.62	6.94
72	11.0	13.8	9.09	7.25
73	10.5	13.2	9.52	7.58
74	10.1	12.6	9.90	8.26
75	9.6	12.1	10.42	8.33
76	9.1	11.6	10.99	8.62
77	8.7	11.0	11.50	9.09
78	8.3	10.5	12.05	9.52
79	7.8	10.1	12.82	9.90
80	7.5	9.6	13.33	10.42
81	7.1	9.1	14.08	10.99
82	6.7	8.7	14.93	11.49
83	6.3	8.3	15.87	12.05
84	6.0	7.8	16.66	12.82
85	5.7	7.5	17.54	13.33
86	5.4	7.1	18.52	14.08
87	5.1	6.7	19.61	14.93
88	4.8	6.3	20.83	15.87
89	4.5	6.0	22.22	16.66
90	4.2	5.7	23.81	17.54

* These figures will change depending on whether a single life or a survivor option is chosen.

provides annuity tables that show the life expectancies the system uses (see table 17).

If you are married, you may figure out a minimum distribution based on the joint life expectancies of your spouse and you. You may also take a minimum distribution based on your life expectancy combined with that of a beneficiary other than a spouse. WARNING! A non-spouse beneficiary will be treated by the IRS as no more than 10 years younger than you are, regardless of his or her actual age. If you are 71 and your beneficiary is a grandchild who is 25, the government will consider that grandchild to be 61 years old for the purpose of figuring the minimum distribution that is required.

One nice thing is that you may refigure the minimum distribution each year to keep step with your life expectancy—until the fund runs out of money. This gives you an advantage if you want to take small distributions and conserve the principal over a long period. If your distributions are based on a joint life expectancy with your spouse, you may recalculate your joint life expectancy each year. But if your beneficiary is someone other than your spouse, you may *not* refigure that person's life expectancy annually; you may refigure only your own, while your non-spouse beneficiary's life expectancy, which was determined as of the year in which you began distribution, will be reduced in later years.

Suppose you are a male who reaches 70½ this year and you decide to make your first withdrawal by the end of the year. Your account balance on December 31 is $75,000, and your life expectancy is 12.1 years. Divide $75,000 by 12.1. $6,198.34 is the minimum withdrawal you must make. The next year, the balance will increase by the interest that the fund has earned, but will be reduced by the distribution you made last year, so your account balance at the beginning of the second year will be $68,801.66 (i.e., $75,000 minus $6,198.34). At the end of the second year, the account balance will be $74,305.79, assuming an 8 percent return on your funds. Your life expectancy, now that you are a year older, will be 11.6 years, so you divide $74,305.79 by 11.6 for a minimum withdrawal of $6,405.67. You can recalculate from there on.

NOTE: In any year in which you do not take your required minimum distribution, an excise tax of 50 percent of the excess in your IRA will be imposed.

Some other things to know:

• If you have more than one IRA, perhaps in each of several banks or other savings or investment institutions, they are all treated as a single contract—including any rollovers. So you do not have to take a minimum amount out of each.

• You report a distribution as ordinary income in the year in which you receive it.

• If you have made contributions to an IRA that were nondeductible (i.e., that came from after-tax money), the portion of a distribution that comes from that money is tax free. How do they figure what that portion is? Let's take an example.

Suppose this year you withdraw $2,000 from your IRA, after making deductible contributions of $6,000 and nondeductible contributions of $10,000 over the last eight years. At the end of this year, the total balance in your IRA account is $22,000, which includes earnings over the eight years. Add the IRA balance at the end of the year and the withdrawal you made, and divide that figure (i.e., $24,000) into the total amount of nondeductible contributions (i.e., $10,000). This will give you 41.7 percent of your withdrawal tax free, with the remaining 58.3 percent (i.e., $1,166) taxable.

IMPORTANT: Record keeping is vital. Be sure to keep copies of Form 8606, on which you list your nondeductible contributions each tax year, as well as your tax returns for such years—plus, of course, all forms (from the banks or other institutions that are holding your IRA savings) that show your contributions to your IRAs and your distributions from them.

CHAPTER 10

Saving and Investing

As we learned in the last chapter, some of the gap you need to fill to be financially independent can be plugged by saving through tax-advantaged plans where you work and other pension plans you can set up for yourself. If any gap remains, and it is likely that it will, you must save and invest after-tax money. Before we examine the specifics that are available to you, let's look at saving and investing in general.

Saving is one thing. Investing is another. There is a big difference between them.

Saving is the foundation of your financial pyramid. You cannot build an investment program unless you first create a solid foundation for it. That means having enough income to meet living expenses, maintain a positive cash flow, and at the same time save a reasonable amount on a regular, continuing basis. It also means accumulating enough money to cover emergency expenses or living expenses for as long as six months if you should become disabled or lose your job—emergency money to buy you enough time to get through a crisis without having to sell your assets or borrow money. In addition, you should maintain a program of saving for one or more specific short-term goals—a new car, a major vacation trip, the wedding of a son or daughter, or anything else you might need in the next 18 to 24 months.

Investing is something else. It is not a get-rich-quick scheme. It is a program—*your* program—to protect the money you save each and every month and, at the same time, put it to work to make more money for you.

To make wise decisions now, you must know the basics of saving and investing. Such decisions will have a strong impact on the amount of money you will have in the future.

Saving asks you to show the discipline to set it up so it is automatic, and then leave it alone so the foundation money accumulates. Investing demands that you take the responsibility for learning some basic concepts so you can achieve a decent return on your money.

If you work for a corporation and participate in any of the defined contribution plans, such as 401(k) or profit sharing, you will most likely be given a choice as to where to invest this retirement money. It is not the responsibility of your employer to advise you on where to invest it. It is up to you—but your employer will give you several options and information about them. The rest of this chapter will give you basic information on savings and investments so you can make educated decisions.

Savings Vehicles

Passbook or regular savings account. This is your good old-fashioned basic savings-bank account. It helps you save money and, at the same time, earn some interest at a very low level of risk. You may withdraw money any time, even through an Automatic Teller Machine (ATM). WARNING: Check the rules of the bank; many impose a service charge every month, which can eat away the interest that is being paid.

Bank money-market deposit account. This one usually gives you a higher yield than a regular savings account. Probably, however, it insists that you maintain a minimum balance. You can write checks against the account. WARNING: Watch out for service charges, and be sure you understand how many checks you are allowed to write each month and whether there is a minimum amount per check.

Money-market mutual fund account. Usually this earns higher interest than a bank money-market account, but, unlike an account in a bank, it is not insured by the Federal Deposit Insurance Corporation (FDIC). Here, your funds are invested primarily in bank CDs and government securities. WARNING: While this account usually provides check-writing privileges, the least you may withdraw with one check is probably $250 to $500.

Certificate of deposit (CD). Financial institutions issue these. They range in length from 90 days to 10 years, and you must keep your money on deposit for the period you have chosen. WARNING: You will pay a substantial penalty for withdrawing a CD before its time.

Treasury bill. This is a short-term loan from you to the federal government. It matures in 3, 6, or 12 months. You buy the bill on a "discount basis" established by the market. For example: You buy a Treasury bill for less than the face value of $10,000. At maturity, you present it for payment of the full $10,000. The difference you receive is the interest paid to you.

Investing

To make your dream come true, investing is imperative. The toughest thing about investing is getting started. Before you get started, you need to figure out your objectives, understand your feelings about investments, and develop a basic grasp of investment "products" and how they work.

Your thinking must be long-term. You don't invest for a month or two. You invest for three to five years down the road—or longer. Your thinking must build in the time needed to recover from inevitable slumps in the market.

Let's face it—investing creates more anxiety and frustration than ever before. Why? For one reason, because the last two decades have seen explosions of new and complex investment vehicles, making it more and more difficult for investors to make informed choices. There is so much information, so many alternatives, such increasing volatility in the market—much of it caused by the way large institutions, trading in huge volumes, dominate the securities market. Their investment decisions can, and often do, cause unpredictable swings in the market. Altogether, it is a gigantic pond and, when you put your toe in at the edge just to test the water, it may seem frightening. Nevertheless, that is exactly what you must do if you are serious about building capital for financial independence.

Let's look at some of the investment objectives you should consider:

Safety of principal. This means protecting your principal from loss. An investment that provides safety tends to have a low rate of return. Examples are U.S. Treasury bills, money-market accounts, savings accounts, and certificates of deposit (CDs). To gain safety, you sacrifice higher yields and, because of inflation, you lose purchasing power: When you liquidate at a later date, your dollar buys less.

Income return. This provides current income on a regular basis to supplement any other current income you have, or to augment your retirement income. Where does it come from? Interest on government, municipal, or high-grade corporate bonds, and from dividends on certain stocks. *Warning:* Especially on long-term income investments, you pay for the privilege of safety by losing purchasing power because of inflation.

Long-term capital growth. To gain financial independence, the name of the game is increase in value over a long period, not current income. What you are looking for is the potential income for some future time and use, such as providing for your children's education or your own farewell to the rat race—i.e., profit or capital gain. You realize the capital gain or increase in value when you sell the investment, so what you are doing is acquiring and accumulating capital for the future, with your money working to earn a profit and keep ahead of inflation. Stocks, stock mutual funds, and real estate are among the best bets for providing long-term capital growth and for hedging against inflation.

Tax minimization. The idea here is to protect your earnings from taxation. The higher your income and the higher your tax bracket, the more important this objective becomes. Investments that can help you meet the objective are, primarily, municipal bonds and *all* the savings vehicles on which taxes are deferred until retirement that are discussed in this book.

Countless factors can influence your objectives. Your age, family responsibilities, tax bracket, current assets and income and liabilities, the amount of money you have available to invest, the length of time you can keep it invested, how you feel about assuming risk—all are determining factors. And don't forget that your objectives are bound to change as time goes by.

Probably, if you are like most people, you have more than one objective. And probably you will diversify your investments among several choices. To help you get a good grasp of your objectives now, go back and review your personal goal sheet in chapter 2. Look particularly at those goals that have time frames of at least three years.

Risk

When you make an investment, you just don't know for sure what is going to happen to it. You take the chance that it may lose money. Every investment involves some degree of risk. In fact, there is a trade-off between risk and return: Generally, they both move in the same direction—the higher the return, the greater the risk. Risk is not, by the way, either boldness or impulsiveness.

What you have to do is find a balance between risk and return that fits your own particular goals. Recognize, first, that your own feelings about risk can get quite emotional, and deal with them. Find a level of risk that lets you sleep at night. Increase your risk tolerance by learning about investment alternatives. And accept the fact that there are some risks over which you have little or no control, but that such risks can be managed. Among the latter are:

Inflation or purchasing-power risk. Whenever you set money aside for a period, inflation will be eating at it during that period. If your investment has a fixed rate of return and inflation is increasing at the same rate, your nest egg will not have grown at all over the period. If inflation is at a higher rate than your rate of return, you will have lost money. Suppose you buy a $1,000 certificate of deposit (CD) that pays 6 percent annually. A year later, you get $1,060. But if inflation has been at 7 percent, your $1,060 will have less actual purchasing power than the $1,000 had when you plunked it down to buy the CD.

How do you counteract the effects of inflation? Invest in common stocks or growth mutual funds that provide a hedge against inflation.

Macroeconomic risk. These are the big worries, typically: changes in the monetary policy of the government, outbreak of a war, changes in the policies of the Organization of Petroleum Exporting Countries (OPEC). Unless you happen to hold high office in Washington, you can do nothing about them (and even if you *do* hold high office, you probably cannot do much about them). Yet every day you run the risk that they may affect your investments.

Market risk. This one is even more worrisome, because it seems closer to you—yet you can do nothing to control it. It is the shifts in the psychology of investors and capitalists that is not related to economic news, yet can cause advances or declines in the market. It includes rumors—the absolute bane of investors—and information that is misleading or false.

Industry risk. Changing circumstances within a particular industry may affect your investments in some corporation in that industry. *Example:* The changes in the automotive industry over the 1970s and 1980s that were brought about by drastic changes in oil prices and the need to make cars with greatly increased fuel efficiency. What is scary is that so many companies are making fundamental changes in their structures and in how they do business.

Business risk. Probably nothing is less predictable than this risk. You buy stock in a company, and suddenly its management changes, or it is merged with another, or acquired by another, or reorganized internally into a new entity. And if none of those things happen, maybe a competitor comes out with a better product, or even an entirely new product, and its stock takes off—leaving yours at a standstill.

Interest rate risk. Since the mid-1970s, interest rates have been on a roller coaster. This makes a problem for investors who bought long-term bonds and want to sell them before maturity, especially if interest rates have since gone up, because the interest rate on a bond is fixed when you buy it. If you want to sell it before it matures, but new bonds with higher interest rates are on the market, no one will want to buy yours—you'll have to discount it and lose some money. If, on the other hand, interest rates are down below the rate when you bought, you can sell at a premium. *Tip:* Buy short-term bonds, or no longer than intermediate term.

If your bond is yielding a high return, you face another risk: that it will be called before maturity by its issuer—if it is callable—after interest rates have fallen, or that it will mature at a time when interest rates are low. Often a bond is called when interest rates have taken a severe tumble and is then reissued at a lower rate. If that happens to you, you have to reinvest the proceeds at the lower rate of interest. *Tip:* To manage this risk, invest in fixed-income bonds or other investments that do not have a call feature. And always buy such investments with a variety of maturity dates.

Liquidity risk. What if there is not enough demand for your investment when you decide to sell it—or when you must sell it to gain cash? Probably nothing is more likely to turn an investor off than the very unpleasant experience of needing cash and finding out that investments must be sold at a loss. The question of whether you can handle the liquidity risk points up the importance of not going into investing unless you have already built up enough liquidity in a savings or money-market account to cover any emergencies or other surprise expenses that might come up in the near future (i.e., within the next six months or so).

Emotional risk. What is your "risk temperature"? No two people have quite the same one. Yet everyone realizes that you cannot make money without taking some risk.

The biggest fear that investors have is the fear of loss. With that fear, they often let emotional decisions lead to costly mistakes, worrying so excessively about money that they panic and sell too quickly when they hear any bad news about their investments.

Closely related is the fear of taking a risk. This fear leads to feelings of inadequacy and to anxiety, with the result that (if you are hit by this fear) you let opportunities slip away. The best way to combat this fear is to do your homework, rounding up all the information you can get on your planned investment, understanding not only its risks but its rewards and how the two balance out, and then making a decision. In sum, never invest in anything until you are satisfied that you know all you can about it.

All of which leads to a review of:

Some Common Investment Mistakes

• *Impatience and unrealistic expectations.* If you expect your invested funds to appreciate from the moment you buy to the time you sell, think again. Remember—the stock market has long been said to be driven by fear and greed. Don't let either one drive you. Price swings are commonplace. When the market is down, you must be patient. Don't get scared and quit the market when it is down. You might miss an opportunity, for that might be just the best time to buy. Buy an investment and stick with it for several years—not just a few months. If you are looking for quick and easy profits, you're expecting too much, but you *can* get rich—*slowly*.

• *Paying too much attention to the market.* Not even the professionals can always time the market accurately to buy when a stock is low and sell when it is high—or before it goes even lower. The best way to make money is to research a stock carefully (or work with a broker who is thoroughly competent). That's why the buy-and-hold strategy is best. It won't allow adverse marketing conditions to affect your strategy.

• *Paying too much attention to what other people are saying and doing.* Tips from friends and neighbors can lead you into investing in what is fashionable. But they are unlikely to give you a portfolio that is oriented wisely to your objectives. Listen to those people if you want a hodge-podge of investments based on hype and glamour, and if you are not all that serious about your declaration of financial independence.

• *Not understanding your investment objectives and the timetable for meeting them.* Remember, investing is a long-term program. If your time frame is limited to one or two years, you are better off putting your money in a bank savings account. But if you have thoughtfully determined your goals, you can choose investments that fit them and meet the level of risk you know you can assume comfortably.

• *Failing to keep abreast of new financial products.* Some people don't seem to understand that new financial products are constantly being introduced. They just stick with the investments they have made, ignoring new products that could better fit their objectives. Read financial magazines and newsletters. Go to seminars. Ask questions of a broker or other financial adviser. Keep yourself informed on why a particular alternative might be a good investment and how it can help you meet your objectives.

• *Failing to make changes.* You are not married to any one stock. When you realize you have a loser, weed it out. Be flexible—not stubborn. Learn to admit your mistakes and take your losses—and get on with it.

• *Failing to understand the investment you are buying.* Don't let a high-pressure salesperson (or anyone else!) talk you into an investment before you understand it. Any good investment will still be around tomorrow, no matter what sales tactics are used today.

• *Failing to diversify.* This is probably the most common mistake. If you put all your eggs in one basket, you are asking for trouble. You could be wiped out if that one investment turned sour. So protect yourself against market changes by diversifying—dividing your investment dollars into various areas so you own a *balanced* portfolio that spreads the risk and limits the potential for a single big loss. This makes you far less subject to the ups and downs of the market. It is one of the most basic principles of risk management. More on this later in this chapter.

Types of Investments

Basically, there are only two types of financial investment: fixed income (also known as a "debt instrument") and equity. When you buy a fixed income investment, usually called a bond, you are lending money to the company or the government that issues the bond. When you buy an equity income investment, you are buying part ownership (no matter how small a part) in a company. Let's take a close look at each.

Fixed Income Investments

Why would you lend your money to a corporation or the government? Because it will pay you interest as long as it has your money, and then repay your money in full when the bond "matures."

The terms of the borrowing arrangement are specified on every bond. The number of years until maturity is known as the bond's "term of maturity." The interest rate is stated as a percentage of the bond's face value. This is called the "coupon rate."

EXAMPLE: A 9 percent rate with a maturity of 10 years means that a $1,000 bond will pay you $90 a year until it matures in 10 years. You will then get back the $1,000 principal that you loaned to the issuer.

What is your risk in buying bonds? A basic rule in the bond market is that interest rates and bond prices move in opposite directions. If interest rates rise, bond prices fall. And vice versa. That means that the actual price you pay for a bond may be above or below its face value, depending on the interest rates at the time when you buy it.

Suppose you buy a $1,000 bond with a 9 percent coupon rate. If the interest rate rises to 10 percent and you want to sell your 9 percent bond, no one will pay you $1,000 for it. The price will drop so that the yield to maturity (i.e., the amount of money you would receive from interest income plus the difference that you paid for the bond and the $1,000 you will) collect will equal 10 percent.

WARNING: With any change in interest rates, the longer the term to maturity, the more volatile the price—and therefore the greater the risk on your part. Why? Because, if interest rates rise above the rate at which you bought, you will be locked into your lower rate of return for many more years than if you had bought a shorter-term bond. For example, if interest rates rise 1 percent, the price of a 10 percent coupon bond with a 30-year maturity will fall about 8.7 percent. If, on the other hand, the interest rate *falls* by 1 percent, the value will rise about 10.3 percent. But if the same bond is maturing in 3 years and the interest rate rises 1 percent, its value will drop 2.5 percent; and if the interest rate falls 1 percent, the value will rise 2.6 percent. Quite a difference between a 30-year bond and a 3-year bond!

Another risk: the loss of purchasing power, due to inflation. The longer you hold a debt instrument, the more likely that inflation will bite a chunk out of it. For instance, if you buy a $1,000 bond maturing in 10 years and inflation is at 7 percent over that period, your bond will buy only $500 worth of goods and services in today's dollars upon maturity.

In addition, don't forget, the interest income you will get over the years is fixed, so it is vulnerable to inflation, too.

If a bond is "callable," it includes a provision that entitles the corporation or government that issued it to re-buy it—or "call" it—at any one of certain specified times and prices. This stipulation helps protect the issuer, who is likely to call the bond if it was issued with a high coupon rate and the interest rates have dropped significantly. If this happens, you must reinvest your money at a lower interest rate.

The various types of fixed-income investments you should know about include:

1. LONG-TERM U.S. GOVERNMENT SECURITIES

All are subject to federal income tax, but not state and local taxes. All are registered, so that income has to be reported to the Internal Revenue Service (IRS).

- *Treasury notes.* These mature in 1 to 10 years. Minimum investment is usually $5,000, which you pay in full when you buy the note. You then receive interest from the government twice a year.
- *Treasury bonds.* Maturity is 10 to 30 years. Available denominations are as low as $1,000. Like Treasury notes, these are bought at full value and give interest twice a year. You can buy Treasuries at any Federal Reserve Bank directly or through the mail. If buying by mail, you must send a certified check a week in advance. Any bank or broker can also sell you Treasuries, but you can expect to pay a sales charge.
- *Government savings bonds.* These pay a floating interest rate. *Series EE* savings bonds mature in 12 years. If interest rates rise, their rates rise. If you hold them for five years, they pay a guaranteed minimum return. The interest is exempt from state and local taxes, and the federal tax on the interest is deferred until the bonds mature or you cash them in. You can buy them in denominations from $50 to $10,000 each, but you don't pay face value. You get them at a 50 percent discount (i.e., a $50 bond costs $25). Buying Series EE bonds is easy: You can order them by calling 800-US-BONDS and charging them to your MasterCard or VISA account, or buy them at banks and other financial institutions. TIP: Buy at the end of the month, since interest is credited from the first day of the month, so you get most of the month's interest as a bonus.
- *Series HH* are issued in four denominations: $500, $1,000, $5,000, and $10,000. You buy them at full face value, and interest is then paid to you semiannually. There is one catch: Series HH bonds may be purchased only in exchange for Series EE bonds. The exchange enables you to put off paying taxes on the accumulated interest on the EE bonds until you cash in the HHs. Meanwhile, the semiannual interest you get from the HHs is subject to federal income tax, but not to state and local taxes.

Government savings bonds are a worry-free investment. But you have certain disadvantages: The yields are lower than from other investments that are almost as safe, such as certificates of deposit (CDs) or Treasury bonds, and they pay only 85 percent as much as five-year Treasury notes. Furthermore, you cannot lock in a high yield. So these are not an attractive investment for gaining financial independence. Think of them, maybe, as savings for your children's education.

2. CORPORATE BONDS

Many companies issue bonds to raise money to help them grow. Usually they pay interest twice a year and range in maturity from 10 to 30 years.

Leveraged buyouts and takeovers have changed the corporate bond market from the staid character it enjoyed for decades. Many of the buyouts of recent years have been paid for with borrowed money, in the form of low-rated or "junk" bonds. Such a takeover clobbers the value of high-grade bonds that were issued before the takeover bid.

How do you know how good a bond is? You check on its rating. Bonds are rated by independent rating services that investigate the creditworthiness of the issuer. Three of the best-known rating services are Moody's Investors Service, Standard & Poor's (S&P), and Fitch Investors Service. Fitch and S&P rate the highest quality bonds with the symbol AAA. Moody's uses Aaa. If you are considering bonds with those ratings, you usually cannot go wrong. Below that but still good are AA or Aa, and just below those ratings comes plain A (the symbol used at this level by all three top services). If you are conservative and don't want to take much risk, you should not buy bonds rated below the A level.

A rating of BBB by Fitch's or S&P, or Baa by Moody's, is still investment grade and carries very little risk. But once you get down to BB or Ba, you are dealing with junk bonds. You pay your money and you take your chances.

The rating is often more important than the name of the company that is issuing the bond. The greater the risk, the higher the interest you can expect (or hope) to be paid. Junk bonds can give you very high yield, but their underlying value moves up and down just as stocks do, depending on the economic news, the rumors, the various "Wall Street" factors.

Convertible bonds are corporate bonds that can be converted into shares of common stock in the same company. They give you the advantage of a bond, which is valuable in a down market, with the growth potential of a stock. What you do is wait hopefully for the company's stock to start climbing, and then convert to it; meantime, you collect the interest income on the bond.

3. MUNICIPAL BONDS OR TAX-EXEMPT BONDS

States, cities, and towns across America issue these to raise money so they can build schools, highways, hospitals, and airports. If you live in the state in which such a bond is issued, you pay no local or state tax on it, and all such bonds are exempt from federal taxes. TIP: Before you buy municipal or other tax-exempt bonds, figure out the tax-equivalent yield—i.e., the yield a taxable bond would have to pay in order to equal that of a tax-exempt issue. Example: Suppose you are in the 28 percent federal income-tax bracket. To better a 7 percent return on a tax-free bond, you would have to find a taxable investment yielding more than 9.7 percent. Of course, you must also take your state's income tax into consideration.

FORMULA

tax-free yield divided by (1 minus your federal tax bracket)
or
7.0 divided by (1 minus 0.28) equals 0.972, or 9.72%

Table 18 shows what a taxable bond would have to yield to equal the tax-exempt return on a municipal bond. Your tax bracket and the interest rate offered by the issuer of the bond will determine which is best for you.

Table 18. Comparing Tax-exempt and Taxable Bonds

With a Federal Tax Bracket of	*A Tax-free Yield of*			
	5%	*6%*	*7%*	*8%*
	Is Equivalent to a Taxable Yield of			
15%	5.9%	7.1%	8.2%	9.4%
28	6.9	8.3	9.7	11.1
33	7.5	9.0	10.4	11.9

4. MORTGAGE-BACKED SECURITY

These are the famous "Ginnie Maes" issued by the Government National Mortgage Association (GNMA). They are mortgage-backed securities—bonds backed by real estate mortgage loans guaranteed by the federal government. The government guarantees to pay you interest and a small amount of principal each month. WARNING: If interest rates drop, homeowners refinance or sell their homes; this can mean that you receive the return of a large amount of principal, rather than a small amount, and you then must reinvest it at a lower rate. TIP: It is important *not* to spend the principal that comes to you as part of each check. Save that for future investments. Note that Ginnie Maes, unlike Treasuries, are fully taxable.

The actual yield on a mortgage security depends on the extent to which the loans that underlie it are paid off ahead of time. Usually, a Ginnie Mae produces a higher yield than a long-term Treasury bond. GNMA certificates come in $25,000 denominations, but you can get Ginnie Maes, in effect, by investing $1,000 or more in a managed fund.

You should know about two other types of fixed-interest investments:

5. ZERO COUPON BONDS

You can buy zero-coupon Treasuries, corporate, or municipal bonds. They are sold at a deep discount. No interest is paid over the life of the bond. Rather, the interest is the difference between what you paid and the face amount of the bond, which is paid out to you upon maturity. So you get no current income, but the longer the maturity, the higher the interest rate. Unless you buy tax-free zeros, you will have to pay income tax each year on the deferred, or "phantom," income—even though you have not received it. Sounds frustrating? What are zeros good for, anyway? They do have a specific purpose: They are for genuinely long-term investment— toward retirement or a child's education.

6. DEFERRED ANNUITIES

These are contracts issued by insurance companies. The idea is to provide you, the buyer of the annuity, with payments at regular intervals starting some time in the future. You can defer that start-up until any date you choose, but the shortest period of deferment you are allowed is five years. WARNING: Most deferred annuities impose a heavy penalty for early withdrawal—usually 6 or 7 percent if you reclaim the money in the first year, then 1 percent less each year until there is no penalty. In addition, if you take the money out before you are 59½, the Internal Revenue Service (IRS) will get a 10 percent excise tax—unless you have died or are disabled.

Your money in a deferred annuity grows on a tax-deferred basis. The interest rate will probably be higher than on short-term government securities, but the interest rate may go up or down. You can, however, lock in an interest rate for 1, 3, 5, or 10 years, as each insurance company offers various lock-in periods and guarantees the interest rate for the period you select. Furthermore, most annuities protect you with a guaranteed minimum rate in case interest rates go down.

When your deferred annuity starts paying you, you will have many of the same choices that are provided when a pension is annuitized (see pp. 81–85). An annuity, remember, gives you a fixed income for as long as you live. Once it starts to pay you, the insurance company guarantees that payment. You cannot get out of the contract—it is irrevocable by either the insurance company or you. The money is tied up forever and, since the payments are fixed, you have no hedge against inflation.

CONCLUSION

Since you are investing for financial independence, you might want to put a small portion of your money into bonds or other fixed-income investments. But remember that this type of investment will not have the same growth potential that equity investments will have (see next section). Also, inflation will erode the value of fixed-income securities.

An annuity is a long-term savings vehicle. Before you buy an annuity, take advantage of other tax-advantaged opportunities that your company offers.

Equity Investments

When you make an equity investment, you *own* something—a part of a company, a piece of real estate, a valuable antique. Let's look at some of the typical equity investments.

1. COMMON STOCK SECURITIES

These make you a shareholder, or part owner, of a corporation. The company pays you income, out of its earnings, in the form of dividends. Common stock is usually a good hedge against inflation. Because there is such a wide variety of stocks available, you can choose from a broad array of risk-return combinations.

Common stock has two disadvantages. If the corporation has to liquidate, you, as the holder of common stock, will be the last to be paid. And if earnings go down, the corporation can reduce or omit dividends. They do not have to be made up in later years.

The fact is, there are no guarantees in the stock market. A company may do well, or it may not. Stock prices change daily. If you are the nervous type, if you could easily be upset by seeing a slight drop in the market price of a stock you own, probably you should not be in the market.

When you are considering buying stocks, you will probably think conservatively. Focus first on successful, financially strong companies whose earnings can be expected to increase. That should mean that their dividends will increase, providing you with current income as they do. Look especially at the "blue chips"—the companies that enjoy a lower-than-average risk of loss of principal or of reduction in income. Blue chips generally are securities of companies that have long histories of sustained earnings and dividends. At the same time, they promise long-term appreciation.

The stocks of newer, smaller companies are more speculative. Such companies are busy plowing their profits back into the company to help it grow, so they pay little or no dividends. But they offer the possibility of substantial capital gains.

Between the conservative blue chips and the speculative investments lies a whole range of other stocks—so many that you should be able to find any number that can meet your specific objectives.

Where do you buy stocks? They are bought and sold—or "traded"—on exchanges. The largest in the United States is the New York Stock Exchange (NYSE). It is where the stocks of major corporations are traded. The American Exchange (AMEX) lists the stocks of smaller, less well known companies. In addition, many stocks are sold "over the counter" on NASDQ or local exchanges. (NASDQ is the National Association of Securities Dealers Automated Quotation.) Any good daily newspaper's business section should give you the listings of the major and regional exchanges. The most comprehensive are published by *The New York Times* and *The Wall Street Journal*.

When you listen to business news on the radio, or see the brief reports that turn up on some TV news, the Dow Jones Industrial Average (DJIA) is always used as an indicator of how the stock market did on that day. The Dow Jones is the trademark of one of the oldest and most widely quoted measures of price movements on the stock market. Its average represents 30 large, seasoned industrial corporations—such names as IBM, Exxon, and AT&T.

Table 19. Stocks versus the Dollar

The Growth of Stocks	*The Decline of the Dollar*

$80

$69.32

70

60

50

40

30

20

10

0

1925   1950   1970   1990

$1.40

1.20

1.00

.80

.60

.40

.20

0

$0.13

1925   1950   1970   1990

SOURCE: *Stocks, Bonds, Bills & Inflation 1991 Yearbook™*. Ibbotson Associates, Chicago (annually updates works by Roger G. Ibbotson and Rex A. Sinquefield). All rights reserved.

Dow Jones also offers indices on the utility and transportation industries.

Standard & Poor's 500 Stock Index is a bigger, broader, more all-inclusive index. Its base is 400 industrial, 40 utility, 20 transportation, and 20 financial issues. It's a good idea to get in the habit of checking to see what each of these key indices is indicating about the stock market, but don't forget that there are some 1,500 stocks listed on the New York Stock Exchange alone.

How do you buy or sell stocks or bonds—literally? You go to a stock broker, or to your local bank. You have to pay your broker or your banker a commission on each transaction, whether you are buying or selling. The commission rate will vary, depending on whether yours is a full-service brokerage or a discount brokerage service. NOTE: Both types of brokers are insured and regulated by the Securities and Exchange Commission (SEC). Discount brokers usually handle your stock transactions at about half the commission

Table 20. How Stocks, Bonds, and Bills Have Performed

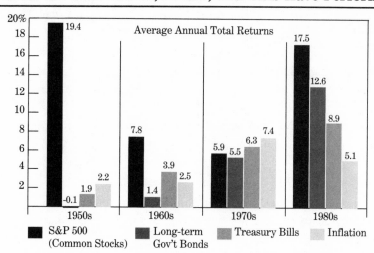

Source: *Stocks, Bonds, Bills, & Inflation 1992 Yearbook*™. Ibbotson Associates, Chicago.

of full-service brokers. Why the lower cost? They do not provide in-house research or the hand-holding, bedside-manner advice you get from a good full-service broker. Rather, they simply handle the trades you tell them you've decided on when you phone them.

THINK LONG TERM   When you think stock market, think long term. This is really important—if you want to kiss the rat race good-bye. Over the years, the stock market has given an impressive performance. For example, during the 1980s the Standard & Poor's 500 Index of common stocks showed an annual average return of 17.5 percent. Compare that with 12.6 percent for Treasury bonds and 8.9 percent for Treasury bills. WARNING: The fact is that the stock market can decline, it can decline quickly, and it can keep on declining for several years. That is why your investment in stocks must be long-term; the longer you hold stocks, the lower the risk.

Risk? Trade-offs? Those may be frightening words, if you are not familiar with investing. Many people are fearful of losing money in the stock market. Rather, they perceive safety in fixed-income savings—money-market accounts, CDs, Treasury bills, guaranteed income contracts (GICs). But they fail to understand that inflation is sure to erode the value of such holdings, especially if they hold them for a long time. Safe can be sorry. Look at it this way: Studies have shown that "it is better to own than to loan."

One dollar invested in a Treasury bill at the beginning of 1940 would have grown to $7.92 by the end of 1989.

One dollar invested at the same time in a long-term government bond would have grown to $8.84.

One dollar invested in a tax-deferred account in the stock market at the same time would have grown to $266.16.

Quite a difference.

2. PREFERRED STOCKS

Like common stocks, these are shares in a corporation; you own a piece of the company. But as the holder of preferred stock, you receive fixed and stated dividends before any earnings are distributed to the common stockholders. The fixed return, however, is not guaranteed. In fact, in some instances, it may not be paid at all. If the time comes when the corporation is to be dissolved, as a preferred stockholder you will be paid before the common stockholders—but you will come after the bond owners. They get their money out first.

3. STOCK OPTIONS

Don't even consider this one unless you have already established a solid base of savings and investments. It is for those who are willing—and in a strong enough position—to take a higher degree of risk. A stock option gives you the right to buy or sell a given number of shares at a specified price. Your option is traded like stocks, but has a specific maturity date that is any time from one day to nine months.

Options are either calls or puts. If you expect a particular stock to rise in value, you buy a call option. It gives you the right to buy the stock at a specified price up to the maturity date. In effect, you pre-fix the price at which you are willing to buy the stock. A put does just the opposite: It gives you the right to sell a stock at a specified price during the option period. NOTE: As the holder of the option, you are under no legal obligation to exercise it.

SOPHISTICATED TIP: You can actually trade only in options, without ever buying or selling the stock. This is a complex maneuver, best done under the advice of a competent stock broker.

4. COMMODITIES

If you are a gambler or a speculator, commodities are for you. You can make or lose a fortune with them. What is a commodity? It is any tangible—silver, corn, pork bellies, orange juice, for example—which is traded on a commodities exchange. When you trade in commodity futures, you buy or sell contracts for future delivery of such commodities. WARNING: Commodity prices fluctuate under the influence of weather, the world economy, and countless other factors you cannot control or, perhaps, even know about, all of which affect the supply of and demand for a particular product. TIP: If you want to have some fun learning about commodities, stop by your video store and rent a cassette called *Trading Places*.

5. PRECIOUS METALS AND GEMSTONES

If this kind of investment turns you on, the first thing to do is find a thoroughly reliable dealer. Investments in precious metals can include gold and silver as well as others. Investment-grade diamonds are the most common gemstones traded. They can be extremely difficult to evaluate—that's why you need a trustworthy dealer. Price fluctuations in metals and stones can be extreme—from wild to worse.

6. REAL ESTATE

Traditionally, real estate has usually been a good investment, whether it is your own home or other land or buildings or both. Depending on when and where you bought it, it has almost always appreciated over time. The recession that began in May 1990, however, found many homeowners holding real estate that had depreciated in value.

Your real estate investment may be in a second, or vacation, home, in apartments or other commercial rental property, or in undeveloped land. You get good tax benefits from owning such real estate. The interest you pay on a mortgage on a first or second home is deductible, provided the amount of the mortgage loan is not more than your purchase price plus the cost of improvements. Taxes on real estate are deductible, too. If you sell your principal residence, your profit (assuming you have made a profit) is not taxed if you then buy another residence of equal or greater value within two years. In addition, if you or your spouse are 55 years old or older, the first $125,000 of profit is sheltered from taxes.

If you own property that you rent to others, you can write off the cost not only of interest on your mortgage but of maintenance, depreciation, and other expenses associated with ownership—up to $25,000 more than your income from rents if your personal income is less than $100,000 and you are "actively" involved in the day-to-day management. If your income is between $100,000 and $150,000, you are allowed to deduct a portion of such costs. WARNING: Managing real estate can be a big responsibility. You have to keep the building maintained, make repairs when things break down, cope with complaints from tenants (not to mention their general idiosyncrasies and lack of respect for the health of your building), and face the possibility that you may not have a tenant in hand when you have space available for rent. And you must pay the mortgage whether your building or apartment or office or loft is rented or not.

You don't have to invest in real estate alone. You can have partners, or you can buy into a Real Estate Investment Trust

(REIT). REITs are sold by some financial institutions and brokerage houses. If you put your money in a REIT, you avoid all the headaches of managing the property. Think of a REIT as an income investment. (It used to be a tax-advantaged investment, but the tax laws have changed.)

WARNING: Compared to other investments, your money invested in real estate lacks liquidity. You run the risk that the market may be down just when it is important for you to sell. Texans who lived through the mid-1980s can tell you about that. So can many people from other parts of the country who have wanted to sell real estate in the late eighties and early nineties.

7. COLLECTIBLES

These include the precious metals and gemstones already discussed. Collectibles really are anything of value that it gives you pleasure to possess—antiques, postage stamps, coins, baseball cards, vintage radios, automobiles, you name it. They will not pay you current income. But if there are many people like you who are interested in the same type of thing, and if that type of thing is rare and becoming more rare every day, you have a collectible that will pay you well if you keep it long enough. Who knows how long is long enough? Only other collectors!

In March 1991, a Honus Wagner baseball card printed in about 1910 was sold at auction for $451,000.

8. VARIABLE ANNUITIES

As its name implies, the return you get from a variable annuity is not fixed. What happens is that the insurance company or mutual fund from which you buy it invests your money in stocks or in a mutual fund. Your return then depends on the performance of the investments in the portfolio. WARNING: Like a fixed annuity you buy well ahead of retirement, a variable annuity demands that you be willing to keep your money invested for a long time.

The variable annuity combines an investment portfolio with tax deferral, and that tax advantage means that you will have to pay the penalties if you withdraw any of your money early—10 percent of the withdrawal if you are not yet 59½, plus income tax on the amount you withdraw.

IMPORTANT: Now that you understand the basics of investing, remember: If you are investing in the stock market, you *must* diversify.

Diversification—the Stairway to Success

If you could describe the ideal investment, it would be stable and liquid and would increase in value by a certain amount within a certain period. Ideal, yes. The only problem is that there is no *one* investment that can meet *all* those criteria.

You can find some investments that provide income, safety, and liquidity—but not growth. Others will give you growth—but not current income. How, then, to achieve the ideal? You must make trade-offs. And you must take some risk to get the opportunity of greater reward. The way you do all this is through *diversification*.

Diversification: Basic to Risk Management

Diversification will not make you a millionaire overnight. But it can make the difference between financial security and losing your shirt. It is one of the most basic principles of risk management or asset allocation. What you do is set up an acceptable level of risk within your portfolio by diversifying in two ways: across industries, and by type of investment. By distributing your money among several different investments, you spread out your risk and you maximize your returns, so that gains in one area tend to offset losses in another.

In this strategy, you balance your portfolio with a number of investments that are not related. Look at stocks and at bonds. They are not related. In an equity-up market (i.e., a bull market), stocks are making money, while bonds and cash are not making as positive a rate of return. Conversely, in a bear market, when equities are losing money, bonds and cash have a more positive rate of return.

Variety is not only the spice of life. It is the key to successful investing over the long term, because neither you nor anyone else can "time" the market with certainty, predicting which way stock and bond prices are going. A variety of assets in your portfolio, each behaving differently, will protect you, so that all of your portfolio is not at risk in a single area of the market. If one investment goes sour, you can rely on another, and a loss in one group of assets will have a limited effect on the entire portfolio.

How to Diversify

You have two basic choices. One is to buy individual stocks and bonds across broad categories. The other is to buy mutual funds, which automatically diversify your investments among a variety of companies and industries. By buying more than one mutual fund, you can further diversify to meet various objectives.

If you are orchestrating your own portfolio, the most important thing is to buy individual stocks and corporate bonds of various companies in various industries. If you are buying municipal bonds, diversify by getting bonds in a variety of geographical locations. Diversify further by buying your bonds with various maturity dates—some short term and some long. Then, if interest rates go down, the yield you have locked in on long-term bonds will be even more valuable and those bonds will appreciate. On the other hand, if interest rates rise, making your long-term bonds suffer, you can be reinvesting your short-term bonds at the higher rate as they mature.

All of these strategies and tactics add up to *balance*—balance through a mutual fund or funds, balance in the portfolio you handle yourself. Balance is what minimizes your risk over the long haul. Balance between taxable and tax-deferred investments, balance between investing for growth and investing for income—your choices can and will make a big difference in how much money you will have in retirement.

As you develop your portfolio, or as you review the investments you have already made in either taxable or tax-deferred savings, remember: You don't have to reallocate for balance all at once. You might start with the money in your 401(k) plan. If it is all in a fixed-income fund, move a part of it into one of the equity funds that are offered. Then ask your company to divide your future contributions (and theirs on your behalf) between the fixed fund and the equity fund. How about your IRAs—where are they now? Probably, if you are like most folks, in a bank certificate of deposit (CD). When the CD matures, check the current interest rate, and think hard about reallocating a part of your IRA funds into a growth investment—especially if your time frame looks ahead at least five years.

Think about Your Investment Philosophy

You have to think about what you think about investing. That sounds like double-talk, but it is true. As you consider how to diversify, make yourself think hard about where you are now and where you want to be in terms of your financial position. What stage of life are you at? What do you want your assets to do for you? You are at a stage where your income from salary is adequate, or even a little more than adequate. Your need for income from investments is low and your time frame is long. You can concentrate on investing for growth. A decade or more from now, you will want to switch to a less aggressive combination of investments, as you will need assets that are more stable and income-producing to cope with the educate-the-kids years and your own financial independence day. Even then, however, you will be smart to keep

Table 21. Check Your Own Asset Mix

Time Category	Your Current Investments	Appropriate Investments	Your Top Three Goals
Short-Term (0–2 Years)	$ _____	Cash	_____
		Money market funds	_____
		Short-term CDs	_____
		Short-term bonds	_____
		Other	_____
Mid-Term (3–5 Years)	$ _____	Intermediate bonds	_____
		GNMAs	_____
		Flexible rate CDs	_____
		High-income stocks	_____
		Other	_____
Long-Term (over 5 Years)	$ _____	Long-term bonds	_____
		Long-term CDs	_____
		Real estate (not including your house)	_____
		Common Stocks	_____
		Hard assets	_____
		Other	_____
Your Total Investments	$ _____		

SOURCE: T. Rowe Price & Associates, Inc.

part of your portfolio invested for growth, so you can keep ahead of inflation.

The mix of your investments is really decided by the mix of your philosophy—your objectives, your age, your time frame, your attitude toward risk, your need for liquidity, your family size, your current income, your current savings. Now is the time to start to develop a long-term strategy so you can kiss the rat race goodbye. Start building capital now to provide the assets that will produce income later on. And remember that bonuses, tax refunds,

Table 22. Find the Investments That Match Your Goals

Time Horizon for Goals	What to Look for	Trade-offs	Investments to Consider
Short-Term (up to 2 years)	• Price that doesn't change or only changes slightly • Maturity of no more than two years • Moderate yields • Regular income payments • Easy access to your money; no withdrawal penalties or redemption fees	• Lower overall returns • Vulnerable to inflation	• Money-market funds • Short-term CDs • Short-term bonds
Mid-Term (3–5 years)	• Moderately high yields • Regular income payments • Price that moves within a fairly narrow range • Bonds: maturity of 3–5 years or flexibility to shorten maturities	• Not as safe as short-term investments • Lower returns than long-term investments • Bonds and Certificates of Deposit (CDs) vulnerable to inflation	• Bonds with intermediate maturities • GNMAs (Government National Mortgage Association securities backed by home mortgages) • Flexible-rate CDs • High-income, conservative stocks
Long-Term (more than 5 years)	• Records of highest long-term returns or highest yields • Capital growth potential • Returns that consistently outpace inflation • Maturity or investment horizon of at least 5 years	• More short-term price swings • Less liquid • Don't invest if you may need to sell out early	• Long-term bonds • Long-term CDs • Real estate • Common stocks • Gold, silver, or other hard assets

SOURCE: T. Rowe Price and Associates, Inc.

and inheritances are monies to be saved. They are lump-sum savings to be invested for your future financial independence.

Confronting your attitude toward risk, and increasing your tolerance toward it, can be handled by starting out in a small way in a mutual fund (see chapter 11).

CHAPTER 11

Mutual Funds

If you are investing in a 401(k) or profit-sharing plan, your company will offer one and usually more mutual funds from which you will be asked to choose. They can range from a fixed-income type fund to one or more stock funds. Because of their lack of knowledge, most people choose guaranteed-income contracts (GICs), which do not provide the long-term growth needed to be financially independent in 10 to 15 years.

In 1979, only 3 percent of American households invested in the nation's 564 mutual funds. Ten years later, there were more than 3,000 mutual funds, with total assets exceeding one trillion dollars, and 25 percent of American households had money in them.

Why such tremendous growth? Because a mutual fund pools the money of many individuals, so each shares in a large diversified portfolio. This spreads the risk. If you are a small investor, it is ideal. In many of the funds, you can make an initial investment of as little as one thousand dollars.

Important Option for Your Defined Contribution Plan

Why should you think about mutual funds? Because they are an important option that you should consider when your company asks where you want to invest the money that is going into your defined contribution plan.

A large percentage of retirement money goes into guaranteed

investment contracts (GICs), which are offered by insurance companies. This is partly because most people invest more conservatively than pension managers do, and partly because options other than GICs are often not adequately explained or well enough understood. As an investor, you yourself may be conservative or aggressive, or somewhere in between, and your employer should offer you options that match your investment philosophy. Your attitude will be directed, probably to a great extent, by your age and the length of time before you retire. (For example, do you have enough years ahead so you can take some risks?) So you need to evaluate all options and decide which meet your objectives.

A mutual fund receives the interest and dividend income from securities it owns. If your fund sells a security at a profit, the gain is usually passed on to you as a capital gain distribution, and the amount you get is in proportion to the number of shares you own. You also profit, of course, if your shares increase in value between the time when you buy them and the time when you redeem them. If the value of the shares goes down, you take a loss.

If yours is a tax-deferred investment, all income and capital gains are automatically reinvested. If it is not, you may choose whether you want to take the cash or buy more shares in the fund. Some funds make distributions monthly, some quarterly, semiannually, or annually.

Besides diversification, you get another advantage: You don't have the responsibility of studying individual stocks and bonds. Professional managers invest the pool of money from the shareholders in a wide variety of stocks, bonds, and other securities from a broad range of industries and government agencies and authorities.

Which Mutual Fund for You?

You do, however, have the basic decision to make: which fund or funds to invest in. A wide variety is out there, many with investment objectives that vary significantly. NOTE: Some are called "a family of funds." That is simply a group of funds that have various objectives, all managed by the same company. Each fund within the family has its own professional managers, who select securities that best meet the particular fund's objectives.

The various types of mutual funds are:

- *Money-market fund.* Also called "liquid" or "cash" fund, this invests typically in Treasury bills, certificates of deposit, and commercial paper that produce high yield.
- *Corporate bond fund, or income fund.* Investing mainly in corporate bonds, it is designed to return a high level of income. Some also invest in preferred stock and U.S. Treasury bonds.
- *High-yield bond fund.* This one buys bonds of corporations that are lower rated, gaining a generally higher rate of return than higher-rated bonds—with a greater degree of risk.
- *Growth fund.* Investing for long-range capital growth, it usually buys common stocks of well-established companies. The primary aim is not current dividends but, rather, an increase in the value of the investment.
- *Aggressive growth fund.* Here, the investment is in industries that are developing and in small companies that have a greater chance for capital appreciation. The objective is maximum capital gains; current income is not a significant factor. That makes this one more risky.
- *Balanced fund.* The balance is between stocks and bonds. The objective is to conserve your capital, give you current income, and promote long-term growth. Other names for this type of fund: equity/income fund, total return fund, growth-and-income fund.
- *Specialized fund.* As its name implies, this fund buys stocks in a single field, such as banking, high technology, health, natural resources, or utilities, but it diversifies by buying from many companies in that field. Some specialized funds invest in commodities or options. WARNING: A specialized fund has a narrow focus. It can be more volatile than the market as a whole.
- *Tax-free fund or municipal bond fund.* Investment is in municipal bonds, appealing to investors in the high-income brackets who seek tax-free income. Some funds buy only bonds issued by a single

state. This gives shareholders who reside in that state the advantage of getting income that is exempt from both state and federal taxes.

• *International fund.* In this fund, you are investing in the securities of companies located outside the U.S., mostly in Europe and Asia. Some investors see this type of investment as a hedge against economic problems in America as well as a way to gain from worldwide economic growth.

• *U.S. government income fund.* Here, your investment is in a variety of government securities, including U.S. Treasuries, federally guaranteed mortgage-backed securities (GNMAs), and other such notes.

No matter which mutual fund or funds you decide on, you can expect any of them to focus on achieving one or more of three main goals:

1. Stability: protection of your principal from risk of loss
2. Growth: increase in the value of your principal through capital gains, when the price increases
3. Income: generation of a steady stream of income

No fund, however, can manage to achieve all three goals. You must recognize that there will be trade-offs. Some funds emphasize only one of these goals, others try to balance two of them. Seldom can any fund give you all three.

How Much Is a Mutual Fund Share Worth?

How many shares you buy depends on the amount of money you are investing, divided by the net asset value on the day you buy them. What is net asset value? It is determined by dividing the total value of all the stocks and bonds that the fund holds by the number of shares owned by all the people who have invested in the fund. The net asset value rises and falls with the market prices of the stocks and bonds held. It is figured daily.

EXAMPLE: If you invest $1,000 on a mutual fund on a day when the net asset value is $13.46, you will own 74.294 shares.

How Mutual Funds Are Taxed

If you put your retirement savings—your 401(k) plan, profit-sharing plan, IRA, Keogh plan, or SEP—into a mutual fund or funds, you will pay no taxes on the interest, dividends, and capital gains until you start withdrawals. Both the money you have put in and the earnings will then be taxed as ordinary income as you take it out. If you are younger than 59½, you will also have to pay the penalties for early withdrawal.

IMPORTANT: If you put money that is *not* retirement savings (i.e., *not* 401(k), profit sharing, IRA, Keogh, or SEP) into a mutual fund, you must pay taxes on all the income, dividends, and capital gains the fund pays you—whether you receive a check or have those distributions reinvested.

Don't Pay Double Taxes

Each January, any mutual fund in which you own shares will send you 1099-DIV and 1099-B forms for the preceding year. It will send copies to the Internal Revenue Service. WARNING: Many investors fail to keep accurate records. They end up paying income tax twice on mutual-fund distributions they have reinvested. You need accurate records that show what you paid for original shares and what you paid later for shares you bought when you reinvested distributions. To avoid double taxation, add the cost of those later shares to your original purchase price. That sum is the cost you report when you are determining a capital gain or loss, after you have sold shares of the fund. (See table 23.)

OTHER THINGS YOU SHOULD KNOW ABOUT
MUTUAL FUNDS AND TAXES:

- It is not only a taxable event when you sell shares, it is a taxable event when you transfer from holdings in one fund to another, even within the same family of funds.
- Figuring how many shares were sold, and what the gain or loss was, is easy when you sell all the shares you have in a fund. But if you sell only some of your shares, it will be assumed that the first in are the first sold (FIFO); in other words, those you've owned the longest are sold first.
- You can, however, specify which shares you want to sell. Your gain or loss will then be based on what those particular shares cost when you bought them.

Put Dollar Cost Averaging to Work

The idea of dollar cost averaging is that you invest a fixed amount of money at regular intervals—usually monthly or quarterly—no matter what the market is doing. If you participate in a 401(k) plan, the deductions from your paycheck each pay period automatically become dollar cost averaging. Over time, dollar cost averaging lets you buy more of your mutual fund's shares when their cost is low, and fewer when the price is up. This tends to reduce the *average* cost per share below what you would pay for a one-shot purchase.

The important thing about dollar cost averaging is to stick with your plan regardless of flutters in the market or the emotions that tempt you to change your strategy. It takes discipline. One way to give yourself that discipline, if you are not in a payroll-deduction plan, is to set up an automatic transfer from your bank account to your mutual fund on a stated day of the month. Make sure the required minimum (probably anywhere from $100 to $250) is no higher than the amount you had planned to invest.

Table 23. Example of Mutual-Fund Records

Transaction Date	Transaction	Dollar Amount	Share Price	Shares This Transaction	Total Owned
2/3	Purchase	1,000.00	74.30	13.459	13.459
10/22	Purchase	750.00	61.72	12.152	25.611
12/24	Cap Gain Paid at 3.59	91.94	58.12	1.582	27.193
12/24	Income Dividend at 1.67	42.77	58.12	.736	27.929
7/08	Cap Gain Paid at 1.38	38.54	70.00	.551	28.480
7/08	Income Dividend at .37	10.33	70.00	.148	28.628
12/22	Cap Gain Paid at 2.78	79.59	67.38	1.181	29.809
12/22	Income Dividend at 3.15	90.18	67.38	1.338	31.147
	Cost Basis	$2,103			

How to Read a Prospectus

When you are deciding which mutual fund or funds to buy, ask for a prospectus on each—and study them. You will find out about the fund's objectives, its past performance, its sales and management fees, and how to buy and sell shares. Some of the details to look for are:

1. *Statement of investment objectives.* What is this particular fund's objective? "Maximum capital appreciation"? It must be an aggressive growth fund. "Income, capital growth, stability"? It is a balanced fund.
2. *Per share table.* What would one share of the fund have earned in each of the past 10 years? Or since the fund was started, if it is less than 10 years old? Remember that earnings include both dividends and capital gain distributions. By examining the table, you can tell whether the fund's performance has been steady or erratic. You will see how it has

done in an up market—and, more important, in a down market. The table may show comparisons with the Dow Jones or Standard & Poor's 500. While it is important to look over the track record of 3, 5, or 10 years, remember that a good track record does not guarantee future performance. Why? Because the market changes. And so do managers of funds.

3. *Fee table.* This tells you what you will have to pay for the service. Check to see whether there is a "load" or sales commission on purchases. A "no-load" fund does not impose an up-front sales charge. (Some mutual funds even bill you for a "re-loading" charge when they reinvest a distribution!) Some fees to watch for and understand:

   a) *12b-1 fee:* applied to the marketing and distribution of funds; can run as high as 1.25 percent annually; assessed by some funds.
   b) *Redemption fee:* used to discourage frequent trading or switching; may be a small flat fee, or a percentage of the redemption price.
   c) *Contingent deferred sales charge (CDSC):* may be imposed if you hold your shares for only a short period; usually a high fee; might be described as a "back-end load" fee as high as 5 percent the first year, 4 percent the second, and so on until there is no fee.
   d) *Operating and management fee:* you pay this as the cost of doing business; expressed as a percentage of the fund's average assets; may average between 0.5 percent and 1.0 percent yearly; this section of the prospectus will also tell you how fees have affected earnings over the last year, and over 3, 5, and 10 years.

4. *Investment policies and risks.* Read this statement with extra care. It describes the risks you will assume as a shareholder, and you must be comfortable with them. It should tell you the kinds of securities—their grade and quality—that the fund usually invests in to achieve its objectives. Look

also for a description of the risks the managers are willing to take, or *not* take, to reach the fund's goals.

5. *Distributions.* Here you will learn how often dividends are paid and when capital gains are distributed, as well as the options you may choose from for receiving them. You should be able to take either or both in cash, or reinvest both, or take one in cash while you reinvest the other.

6. *How to buy and redeem shares.* What is the lowest amount you may invest to start an account in the fund? How about subsequent investments—what's the minimum? Can you make telephone transfers, or take advantage of dollar cost averaging? This section should give you all the answers on procedures for buying and selling shares.

Advantages of Mutual Funds

Among the many advantages of putting your voluntary savings toward retirement into one or more mutual funds are these:

• *Low minimum investment.* It doesn't cost you an arm and a leg to get into a mutual fund. Each sets its own minimum for an initial investment. Most want somewhere between $250 and $1,000.

• *Professional management.* Probably you don't have the time or resources—and maybe not even the inclination—to study the continuing economic changes that affect the securities market. Nor should you. Professional managers are in the business to make intelligent decisions about the securities in the fund's portfolio, based on their research. They study the trends, keep up with a daily stream of financial information, even travel to visit company plants and talk with executives to get insight into the viability of various stocks and bonds.

• *Easy record keeping.* Mutual funds are noted for their convenient record keeping. Any time you make a transaction, you can expect a confirmation statement. Regular year-to-date statements of your account should come every month or quarterly. An end-of-the-year statement, along with forms 1099-DIV and 1099-B for reporting income and capital gains should come along in plenty of time for you to do your tax return.

- *Automatic reinvestment.* To keep your account growing, you can instruct the fund to reinvest your income and capital gains in additional shares.
- *Automatic withdrawal.* If you want to get regular cash income, you can set up an automatic withdrawal system with the fund, including direct deposit to your bank account. This can be particularly convenient in your retirement years.
- *Liquidity.* Mutual funds are liquid. Any time you want to sell, the fund will buy back its shares—at a time, you hope, when you will realize a gain rather than a loss.
- *Convenience and flexibility.* Since many funds are actually a "family" of different funds, they can let you switch from one to another as your needs and objectives change, or as you want to take advantage of changes in the market. This is known as "investment timing." In many funds, it takes only a telephone call to switch funds or to redeem (i.e., sell) shares.
- *Diversification.* Each share you buy in a mutual fund gives you an interest in a wide range of stocks, bonds, or other kinds of investment—whatever the fund specializes in.

CHAPTER 12

Non-Income-Producing Assets

Many people tend to forget how much money they have invested in assets that do not produce any interest or other income. Often they also ignore the possibilities that such assets provide for helping them in later years. Among such assets are fine art, collections of coins or stamps or baseball cards, antiques, jewelry, automobiles, to name just a few. If you plan to kiss the rat race good-bye at the age of 45 or 50, you might want to consider selling some of your collections, investing the money, and using that money for living expenses or to help start up your new career. You might consider this before you tap into tax-deferred investments.

If you are like most people, you have one non-income-producing asset that is also most likely to be the greatest in value: your home. You have worked hard to make it the comfort and joy and base of security that it is. You may find it well worthwhile to consider converting it into an income-producing asset. How? By selling it and changing to living quarters or a life-style that cost less while you invest the difference—the money you take out or save, or both—in any of the investment options we have already discussed in this book.

The first question, of course, is: Where do you go? Maybe you relocate to another suburb, or another neighborhood, near where you live now—but one where the housing costs less. Maybe you relocate to another part of the country—not impossible if you are stepping off the corporate treadmill and reorganizing your life.

Before you decide to relocate—whether across town or across country—get all the information you can. Visit the area. Poke around. See what the homes are like, but also the shops, the drugstore and cleaner and lunchroom, the schools if you have children not yet out of high school. If the climate will be different, check it out at its worst time of the year. Can you take the heat and humidity of a Florida summer? The windy chill of a Maine winter? How about the cultural activities, the arts, the community theatre, the galleries? And the recreation—boating, fishing, golf, tennis, hunting, skiing—will you be happy with what you find there?

Don't be shy about talking to strangers when you are checking out a possible new home town. At the gas station, the supermarket, anywhere along the sidewalk—find out what they like and don't like about the town and its facilities. And be sure to dig into whether or not some impending event or issue is about to push local taxes to a new high.

Unleash the Equity in Your Home

Among the many things to think about when you are debating whether to sell your home is how much it *really* costs to maintain this non-income-producing asset. Aside from the monthly mortgage payment, how much goes into heating oil or gas, garbage removal, electricity, painting indoors and out, plumbing repairs, property taxes, homeowner's insurance, and fertilizing the lawn so it will grow faster so you can pay the kid next door (or your son) more often for mowing?

What if? What if you moved to a home where all those costs were less—or were removed entirely? What if you lived where you could walk out, lock the door, and be away for two or three months without worrying about repairs, pipes freezing, or lawn mowing and snow shoveling? What if you moved to a smaller single-family house, with lower taxes, lower cost of maintenance, but with your own piece of land to dig in and putter around on? What if you moved into a condominium unit, where one carrying charge covers all maintenance of the exterior of the house as well as the grounds and you maintain only the interior? And aren't there other "what if's" to think about?

Some Housing to Consider:

• *A smaller single-family residence.* If you are a homeowner now, you know about the fringe expenses beyond the mortgage— all the maintenance costs, taxes, etc., just mentioned above. If you move to a smaller house in a less expensive neighborhood, these costs will probably be reduced, but they will not go away.

• *Condominium.* This can be a unit in a high-rise building, an attached townhouse, or even a separate home (in cluster housing), and it can be ideal for people who are retiring. You own the unit you live in, and you pay a "common charge" or "carrying charge" to the condominium association to cover your share of the cost of maintenance of all the common areas—lawn, snow removal, interior lobby and hallways (if any), and of the roof and exterior walls. Your ownership of the unit gives you also a proportionate interest in the common facilities.

WARNING: Common charges can escalate. Special assessments can be levied—to pay for major repairs or maintenance problems. Recreational facilities—the swimming pool, the tennis and racquet-ball courts—can become run-down. Infighting can occur among the board of directors who run the condominium and, like you, are owners in the complex. So check out the maintenance and the recreational facilities. Look at the record of increases in carrying charges in the past. Talk to the residents. Find out what they like and don't like—maybe even *whom* they like and don't like.

• *Cooperative.* This is different from a condominium. A nonprofit corporation owns the unit you live in. You buy shares in the corporation, and the value of your shares is proportionate to the value of your unit. You and all the other owners make monthly payments to the corporation, each paying according to the number of shares you own. The payment covers property taxes, maintenance, and your share of the mortgage (if any) on the building. When you want to sell your apartment, you are really selling shares in the corporation.

• *Mobile home.* A "mobile home" is not usually "mobile" at all. It is a fully equipped home built in a factory and trucked (you've passed more than one "wide load" on the interstate) to a permanent site. Kitchens and bathrooms are contemporary, interiors are roomy and luxurious, fireplaces and porches or decks are not uncommon. You may find that you can choose between renting or buying the land your mobile home sits on. This is probably the least expensive form of home ownership. Often a mobile park includes shopping and recreational facilities—swimming pools and rooms for card-playing, exercise, and hobbies.

• *Renting.* If (or when) you sell your home, think seriously about banking the entire amount you get for it—less your mortgage repayment if the house has not yet been paid off. Then rent an apartment or a house, especially if you are moving to another area of town, another town nearby, or—even *more* especially—if you are going to an entirely different geographic area. Renting is a wonderful way to try out an area and a life-style.

It is also wonderful for people who do not want to be tied down in one place and don't want the responsibility for financing or maintaining a house, or don't want to own an apartment. It lets you move when you want to, or when your lease expires, without waiting around to sell. And you get no surprises—no hidden costs, no sudden plumbing bills—when you rent. WARNING: Most landlords expect to increase the rent when they renew the lease.

• *Motor home.* This one *is* mobile. Here today and gone tomorrow. You can roam around at will, park here a day, there a week, as the spirit moves you. Some retired people spend much of the year doing just that, with a rented apartment and a post office box as the home base. WARNING: This is a life-style you want to be sure about. Rent a motor home several times, in various seasons. Get a feel for a month's stay in a camper park. See if you can discipline yourself to have a place for everything and everything in its place, just as those do who live in the cramped space aboard boats. Valerie and Eric, whom you'll meet a little bit later, use what they call a camper to go between New Hampshire and California.

• *Boat.* This is like the motor home—you live in tight space, and you go when you want to go. Some early retirees spend several months of the year aboard boats and love every minute of it. If you are a good sailor now, own a boat, spend every spare moment on it, and spouse and family have sea legs, too—go for it.

Moving costs money, as well as disruption and resettling. Some of the hidden costs are the commission to your real estate agent or broker, legal fees, the moving van and movers, fresh carpeting and drapes at the new place, and perhaps such other items as lamp fixtures. If you are planning to relocate to another part of the country, get several estimates on moving and storage charges. If it has been a while since you moved, you may be in for a shock.

Moving and State Taxes

Before you decide to move to another state, check out the taxes. Write to the state department of taxation and get resident tax forms. Fill them out, or have your accountant do it, and see what your tax liability would be if you lived there.

Florida is the place to be, no question about it—from a tax standpoint. The state gets most of its revenue from its sales and gasoline taxes. It has no income tax. Property taxes are lower than in most other states. A move to sunny California, on the other hand, will probably double your state taxes. You will pay income tax there, and you will find property taxes high compared with other states.

If you do move to another state, be sure to avoid having two states make claims on your income. Establish the new state as your permanent home immediately—register to vote, get your driver's license, transfer your auto registration and bank accounts. File a tax return in the new state. Change your will so it cites your new residence. If you maintain a home in your former state, keep careful records that prove you are spending the majority of your time in your new state.

SOME QUESTIONS TO ASK ABOUT THE NEW STATE:

1. Will it tax your Social Security benefits?

2. Does it tax interest, dividends, and capital gains? If you are moving to a state with a higher capital gains tax, time your asset sales so you sell any that you plan to sell *before* you move. And don't forget that if you hold municipal bonds in your present state, where they are tax free, they may be taxed by your new state.

3. How about taxes on your pension? If you are getting a monthly check, income taxes are probably not withheld. That means your pension money will be considered taxable income under state rules. WARNING: Lump-sum distributions have been a problem in some states—they tax withdrawals from rollover IRAs of former state residents who move out of the state and then begin withdrawals, as well as such withdrawals by new residents who earned their money in other states. Then, if the new resident pays state taxes in his or her former state, they allow a credit. California has been tracking down former residents who moved out of state. Other states that impose similar taxes are getting better at finding people who move away and take lump-sum distributions.

4. What about estate taxes? Some states impose a heavy inheritance tax. Others have none. Often the tax depends on whether your heirs are spouse or children.

State tax laws have a way of changing as frequently as federal laws. Before you relocate, spend some time doing your homework on state tax rules. Concentrate especially on what can happen in the year when you move. Take nothing for granted. Check it out.

TIP: Don't put your house on the market until you are really sure what you will have to spend on a new home—the kind of new home you are certain you want. If the profit potential is not as great as you thought it might be, trading down may not be the answer.

Check the tax consequences of your proposed move, too. If you are 55 or older, the federal government allows you an exemption of $125,000 on your capital gain on selling your home. The exemption has some strict rules:

- This is a *one-time* exemption. You are not allowed to take it more than once, and neither you nor your spouse may have used it before. If, for example, a husband and wife use the tax break, are later divorced, and then marry other people, none of the four will be able to use the tax break on the later sale of some other house or houses.
- Only one spouse must be over 55—either one of you.
- You must have owned the house for five years, and it must have been your principal residence for at least three of the five.
- If your gain on the sale of the house is more than $125,000 and if you use the gain to buy another home of at least equal value that is your primary residence, you do not have to pay taxes on the gain.

EXAMPLE: Suppose you bought your home for $100,000, and now you sell it for $225,000. You pay no tax as long as either you or your spouse is at least 55 years old. Upon the sale for $225,000, you can buy another house at a lower price and keep the difference to invest for the future.

Family of Do-It-Yourselfers Make a Killing

A skilled do-it-yourselfer who worked full-time in marketing and sales, Eric bought a shorefront house in Connecticut in 1976 for $120,000. It was in disrepair, inside and out, but structurally sound. With his wife and two sons, he got the house in shape, clean and sparkling. In 1984, they rented the house to a Wall Street yuppie for two months while they occupied a friend's apartment in New York and vacationed in a condo in California, their native land.

The next winter, Eric was laid off. Too young to get an enhanced pension, he nevertheless walked away with $85,000—one year's salary. He and Valerie had little else in savings. Always the realist, Eric said, "Okay, we'll sell the house." They did have somewhere to go: During the good years, they had bought a small one-bedroom condo on a ski slope in New Hampshire, and they still owned another in California, bought 15 years earlier when they were living in the west.

Just then, the Wall Streeter called about renting the house again over the summer. Eric, the ultimate salesman, offered to sell him the house for $750,000. No, said the Wall Streeter. "As is," said Eric, meaning that he would include everything in it except the family's personal mementos and clothing. Yes, said the Wall Streeter. "When we walked out with our toothbrushes," he said, "the beds were made, linens were in the closet, china in the hutch, pots and pans in the kitchen, teapot on the stove."

Selling the house enabled Eric and Valerie to pay off the $105,000 mortgage and bank nearly $645,000. "The interest rates were still good," says Eric, "so we put some of the money into short-term CDs and some into longer-term bonds. Then we took off for New Hampshire—moved into less space than that big old house, but we could live very cheaply. We just cut out the nonessentials." They also rented the condo at Christmastime for a tidy sum and went west for the winter.

By the following fall, the real estate market in New England was beginning to come apart. Eric watched the ads. During the winter, he found a builder who was stuck with a contract to build a house for yuppies who were no longer yuppies and could no longer afford the house. Eric worked out a deal before the bank foreclosed—bought the house for $175,000 in cash, sold the condo for what they had paid for it, used some of their cash to furnish their new home, and put money into a reserve fund to pay the capital gains tax that was coming due on the sale of the house in Connecticut. (Although they had reinvested the proceeds from that sale within the two years required by the IRS, they still had to pay some tax because they had not bought a house of at least equal value.) By the time all the dust settled, Valerie and Eric had about $400,000 still invested and producing income for them to use.

"We spend half the year in New Hampshire," says Valerie, "and half in California. We started a business together that we can run from wherever we are—importing foodstuff from Europe. With the computer and the FAX and call forwarding, we have everything the business needs."

Now she and Eric cross the country twice a year in a camper, their computer disks with them. "We've seen a lot of the U.S.A.," says Eric, "by using various routes back and forth. The camper saves us on meals and motels, and we're having the time of our lives."

Sell That Second Home?

If you have a vacation or weekend home at a lake, in ski country, or at the shore, are you using it as much as you once did? Has the cost of keeping it up gone wild? Is the expense of owning it justifiable? Chances are, it is tough to rent, and if you do rent it you then have to be an absentee landlord, managing it by remote control. No fun. It may hardly be worth the cost of insurance and property taxes for what you get out of it.

If all that sounds like your second home, it is time to sell it and put the proceeds to work producing income.

CONDOS NORTH AND SOUTH: On a hunch, Sandy bought some undeveloped land in Connecticut in 1976 for $55,000. Nine years later she sold it for $110,000. With the profit, she and her new husband, George, bought a condominium in Florida, then another in Vermont. The Florida place has been rented out ever since. George took early retirement in 1982, when he was 51, and Sandy in 1991 when she was 53. Now they plan to sell both condos and invest the money, thus avoiding the landlord headache and the Vermont upkeep.

Tap the Equity in Your Home?

Some people are property-rich but cash-poor. They bought their homes years ago for what seem today like phenomenally low prices. Over the years, such homes have appreciated substantially, so the owners have a large amount of equity in them. Equity is the cash value of your home minus whatever you still owe on it. For instance, if you bought your house for $50,000 and it is worth $200,000 today, and if you have only $20,000 left to pay on the mortgage, you have $180,000 in equity in your house.

Traditionally, that has been money you could not get at. You had to sell the house if you wanted to get the equity out of it. But today there are several ways you can tap the equity in your home without selling it. Some, however, can be used only in the traditional retirement years.

1. Reverse Annuity Mortgage (RAM)

You can turn the equity in your home into an annuity income without selling the house. This is a relatively new idea, and each state has been developing its own guidelines. The basic system is this: A bank or other lending institution takes a lien on your house and buys an annuity that is equivalent to the amount of equity you have in it, and that will pay you every month. The amount of your monthly check depends on your age, your equity, the interest rate, and the length of the loan. The life of the annuity may be as long as you live, as long as you and your spouse both live, a specified length or term (as short as 5 years or as long as 20 or more years), or until you sell the house. When you sell it, you repay the loan from the proceeds—or your executor repays it, with the balance going to your estate.

WARNINGS:

- Don't get into this one—don't even consider it—without sound financial advice.

- If you set up a RAM for a fixed period, you may outlive it. Will that then be a problem?
- Depending on both the value of your home and the region where you live, the maximum RAM you can get is from $67,500 to $124,875. That means, for example, that if you have $100,000 in equity you could get about $234 monthly for the rest of your life, starting at age 65. Wait till you are 85 and you'll receive about $604 a month.

Other things you should know about RAMs: The shorter the term you set, of course, the higher the monthly payment. The Federal Housing Administration (FHA) does insure mortgages made by private lending institutions. The start-up costs in establishing a RAM are stiff.

2. Sale/Leaseback Arrangement

Consult a lawyer who specializes in real estate before you seriously consider this option. Here's how it works. You sell your house to someone who leases it back to you for your lifetime, or the lifetimes of you and your spouse. The most likely people to sell it to? One or more of your children, who make a down payment and establish a mortgage either with a lending institution or directly with you. You and the new owner agree on a reasonable rent for you to pay. The buyer pays all taxes, insurance, and maintenance, and gains the tax advantage of deducting the interest paid on the mortgage. If you take back the mortgage (i.e., you, rather than a bank, hold the mortgage), you will get the monthly payments directly as the buyer pays it off. That, minus the rent you are paying, should give you positive cash every month.

The buyer might also purchase a deferred payment annuity for you, providing for continuing monthly income once he or she (or they) have paid for the house. In that case, upon your death, the house would not be a part of your taxable estate.

3. Home Equity Line

You can set up a line of credit secured by a lien against your home, then draw on it by writing checks or using credit cards. Remember that repayment is not deferred. For details, see chapter 5.

DEE COULD TAP EQUITY A DIFFERENT WAY: Pondering how to improve her cash flow, Dee is thinking of a way to keep her lovely family home in California, yet gain some capital. Her plan is to sell a share of the equity in the house. Her accountant has seen a client through the process. Her thinking is that this could be an option when she is ready to retire from the airline in 10 years or so.

What Else Can You Tap?

Your house is not the only non-income-producing asset you can tap to produce cash if, as, or when you are shifting gears into a new way of life. Think about your *collectibles*—the postage stamps and coins, jewelry, fine art and antiques, books, baseball cards, comic books, dolls, whatever. Are you trapped by them? Are some out of sight in a safe deposit box because you are worried about burglars? Is the cost of insurance getting out of hand? Maybe the time has come to pare down.

The dilemma, of course, is that you are torn between the sentimental reasons for holding onto such possessions and the practical reasons for liquidating them so you can put the money into income-producing investments. If you decide to sell them, consider getting them appraised. Always work with a reliable dealer. You might not be the owner of a baseball card worth $451,000, but 10 or 12 less rare cards at a couple of hundred bucks apiece can bring you a nice bundle of cash.

Don't forget the tag sale. Any couple who have been in the same house for 20 or 30 years can put on "the mother of all tag sales" and take in at least a couple of thousand dollars—enough to take care of a good part of the cost of moving.

WORKSHEET X: NON-INCOME-PRODUCING ASSET EVALUATION

Non-Income-Producing Assets	Net Sale Value	Cost of Ownership
Personal Residence		
Recreational Property		
Cash Value Life Insurance		
Home Furnishings		
Automobiles		
Jewelry		
Antiques		
Coin or Stamp Collection		
Fine Art		
Other		
TOTAL		

MARTY AND FRED netted seven thousand dollars on their tag sale—not including the sale of some fine antiques. They sold their home, which was quite expensive to maintain, moved into a condo that they had purchased in the same town several years earlier and had been renting out, and bought a boat that they now use like a summer cottage.

Sometimes you change your mind. Sue and Don bought property on a lake in North Carolina several years before his retirement date. They expected to sell their home in the greater New York area and build down south. But by the time Don retired, they found that they wanted to stay put.

Their revised plan: They'll try to buy a one-bedroom apartment in the Washington, D.C., area, where all their children have settled. That way, says Sue, "We can visit them and not feel like guests. We'll have our own place to stay in."

Fill out worksheet X, about your non-income-producing assets. The net sale value is what you will actually expect to receive from the sale of your house or of collectibles. Don't forget that you have to pay for appraisals or that you will most likely have to pay a commission to a real estate broker. Under Cost of Ownership, be sure to include insurance, utilities, maintenance, and property taxes—figures that you should have in your completed Cash Flow Statement.

CHAPTER 13

Investing for College

While you are thinking about getting out of the rat race, you may have children who will be ready to go off to college at about the same time. The one thing that is obvious is that good planning and starting early will make a huge difference in accumulating the amount you must come up with by the time your child starts college.

How Some Parents and Students Did It

While Eric and Valerie were still living in their "sweat equity" Long Island home, their two sons were enrolled in a private college nearby. They lived at home, saving on dormitory costs and meals, and worked part-time to pay for all their expenses.

At the same time, Howie and Nora sent their two sons to one of their state colleges, so tuition costs were low. The boys also worked part-time to pay for all their expenses—books, student activities fees, field trips, lab fees, etc.—except the tuition.

Andy used a different method. As each of his children was born, he started buying U.S. savings bonds through the payroll savings plan. He liked this "painless" way of saving for education, because the money came out of his paycheck before he got it twice a month. He never saw the money.

What College? When? How Much?

Let's agree that nothing is as unpredictable as a child's future interests and needs. If you have young children, or even if they are already into adolescence, who can say where they will want to go to college or how many years they will spend in the academic world or how much they themselves can pay through student aid, scholarships, or summer jobs? But you must start somewhere. So think about what kind of school they may go to—public? private? local community college? Then figure out the cost, and project it out to the year when your child will start.

If your state university now costs $10,000 a year and your child will be entering 13 years from now, it will then cost $21,400 a year—assuming a 6 percent increase each year until then. That means you must invest for long-term growth, and you must seize every tax advantage you can get your hands on.

SOME THINGS TO KNOW ABOUT TAXES AND SAVING FOR COLLEGE:

• For a child under 14 years old, the first $550 of unearned income is tax free, the second $550 of unearned income is taxed at the children's rate of 15 percent, and any unearned income above $1,100 is taxed at the parents' rate.

• After your child reaches 14, all earned as well as unearned income will be taxed as if your child is an adult. Obviously, your child's taxes will be substantially lower than yours.

• The interest on U.S. savings bonds, if you hold them for more than five years, is tax deferred until you redeem them. If you wait to redeem them until your child reaches age 14, all the accumulated interest will be taxed at the children's rate, rather than at your higher rate. The bonds must be issued in your name or jointly with your spouse. TIP: You may exclude from your income all or part of the interest you receive when you redeem U.S. savings bonds if you are using them to pay for tuition and fees (but not for room and board or courses involving sports or games that are not part of a degree program) at an eligible educational institution. For the interest to be tax free, the total you cash in may not be more than the tuition and fees you have to pay for the year. If you cash in more, you must pay tax on the difference. But WARNING: There is a phase-out if your modified adjusted gross income is between $60,000 and $90,000 (for married couples filing jointly) or between $40,000 and $55,000 (for all others). Once you reach $90,000 (or $55,000), you get no tax break. Watch for continuing changes in these rules.

• You must pay taxes on the income from zero-coupon bonds each year, even though you do not receive any income directly. (Zero-coupon bonds are the ones that have been stripped of their interest coupons. They are sold at a deep discount, and when you buy them you know exactly how much you will get when they mature.) TIP: Instead, buy *municipal* zero-coupon bonds; their interest is not taxable by the IRS—states, however, may impose their own taxes.

WARNING: If you are buying bonds, be sure to match the maturity dates with the time when you will need the money for tuition.

Where you put savings for education depends to an extent on the current ages of your children. If they are quite young—say, still at least 10 years away from college—you want long-term growth and appreciation. Buy that kind of investment, and don't even think about dividends. Mutual funds are ideal. Most of them will automatically transfer money from your checking account every month or every quarter, so you are putting money into the fund on a regular basis. When your child reaches 14, you can then sell the shares and move the money into a safe, income-oriented investment.

Life insurance is another tax-deferred way of saving. If you buy a whole, or universal life, policy, cash value will build up. The policy will protect your family if you should die prematurely, and meantime you gain a sound savings plan for your child's education. After your child is 14, you can borrow the cash value and put it into a savings or money-market account from which tuition will be paid. Or, if you would rather not turn over the funds, let them accumulate until the first tuition payment is due.

> **TIP:** As a parent (or as a grandparent), you can set up a custodial account under the Uniform Gifts to Minors Act (UGMA). As custodian, you are responsible for managing the account until the child reaches maturity (at age 18 in some states, 21 in others). The child can then do whatever he or she wants to with the money—go to college, go on a trip around the world, or go on a spree. An account of this type is allowed to earn as much as $1,100 in interest annually before the earnings are taxed.

Another thought: Consider creating a *trust* under Section 2503(c) of the 1986 Tax Code. The trustee—usually the parent or grandparent—has complete control over both the principal and its earnings until the child reaches 21. The trust pays income tax on interest and dividends at its own rate, thus avoiding the "kiddie tax" rules, with the first five thousand of income taxed at 15 percent and any amount above that at 28 percent.

> **WARNING:** Putting money into an account in your child's name seems like a great idea when kids are tots and college is off beyond the horizon. But later on, when college is near, you may be applying for financial aid. Most college financial aid people earmark 5 to 10 percent of the parents' assets for annual college costs. But they earmark 35 percent of any assets held in the name of the student. So don't be too eager to transfer money to an account in your child's name. Think it through.

What If You Haven't Saved Enough for College?

Financial aid offices at colleges are helpful in telling applicants what is available. You will find that the federal government provides billions of dollars in grants and loans. Get the information on them and study it, so you know all you can about what is offered and how you can help your child to qualify for a grant or loan. IMPORTANT: Study them now. But then *keep up to date.* Some of the rules, policies, and dollar amounts are sure to change before you deliver your child at the campus gate.

When you apply for financial aid, retirement accounts, though listed on financial aid forms, are usually not considered available as sources of educational funding. However, the current financial aid form asks that you list under unearned income the amounts that you have contributed to any retirement accounts, but only for the current year. This is certainly another reason to take advantage of every kind of retirement account.

Many state education departments, and many private colleges and universities, are coming up with their own ideas for helping. Some offer loans with repayment over as long as 20 years. Some offer *prepayment* plans. In these, you pay for tuition in one lump sum, before your child enters, at a discounted fee. The cost will then be based on when your child will enter and how much the college figures it can earn on your money between now and then. The theory is that the interest will make up the difference between today's tuition cost and what will be charged at the time of your child's arrival. Some states offer prepayment plans at the state universities, and some offer special bonds that are exempt from state taxes and that may be used as a form of prepayment of tuition at any public or private college within the state.

The plan leaves some questions to be answered:

- What happens if the school cannot earn enough return on the investment to meet the future costs—will you have to come up with the shortfall?
- What happens if your child decides not to go to that college? How much of a refund do you get?
- What happens if your child doesn't go to college at all?

Another source of funds, if college is just around the corner and if you have good equity in your home, is to take out a *home equity loan.* This has one particular advantage over other loans: The interest you pay on the first one hundred thousand dollars of the loan is deductible from your income tax.

Don't forget another source of funds: the future student. Baby-sitting, lawn mowing, paper routes, supermarket bagging and checkout, snow shoveling, serving up Big Macs and fries, house-painting, car washing—there's no end to the ways in which high-school students, as well as college students themselves, earn money for college. A student who works full-time in the summer and part-time after school hours can handle a substantial part of the responsibility for college costs.

With those costs in the stratosphere, many parents tell their children flat out that they will pay only for a state school, since the expense is about half of what a private college costs. Others opt for a private college that is nearby, so the child can live at home. Still others, if they can—and this could be an important consider-ation for your long-range plan—decide to pack up and move the entire family to a state like California, Michigan, or Wisconsin that provides a top-notch system of state colleges and universities.

CHAPTER 14

Insurance

Who Needs It?

Life Insurance

Think of life insurance as playing three roles: First, it protects your family by becoming a source of regular income if you die. Second, it builds up savings that you can use to help educate your children or when you become financially independent. Third, it can pay your estate taxes.

Do You Need Life Insurance?

Ask yourself these questions:
- Is my income needed to maintain my family's life-style?
- Do I have dependent children?
- Do they need my income to help pay for their educations?
- Do I own my own home? Is there an outstanding mortgage?
- Do I have a lot of outstanding debts?
- Do I have little or no savings?

If your answer to one or more of these questions is "yes," you need life insurance.

If you have a *family*, you need life insurance—especially if it includes young children. Just about every young family has shouldered tremendous financial responsibilities that are sure to continue at least until the youngest makes his or her farewell appearance in cap and gown with the ultimate advanced degree in hand. But very few families have enough assets built up to provide the income needed to replace a lost salary. Could your family meet its monthly fixed expenses without you?

Or, for that matter, if you and your spouse are both working full-time to keep up the family life-style, could you maintain that level if your spouse's income stopped? If both of you are working, both of you should be insured. Not only that, but if one of you is a full-time homemaker, insurance is needed. Without the homemaker, insurance benefits can provide the cook, the housekeeper, the gardener, the important child care at least until the youngest is in high school.

If you are a *single parent*, you need life insurance for all the same reasons—to avoid leaving other family members with the huge financial burden of providing daily care, as well as college money, for years to come.

If you are a *working couple without children*, you might need life insurance, too—especially if you have a number of outstanding debts or very little savings—to take care of such expenses as long-term care, final illness, and funeral costs. (Nobody likes to bring up this subject, but it has to come up sooner or later. There is no time like the present, since we are talking about life insurance.)

Your needs will change over time. As your children grow up, leave home, get out on their own, and as your assets increase at the same time, you should be able to cut back on insurance coverage.

How Much Insurance Is Enough Insurance?

It's rather easy to tell how much life insurance you need. You should have enough so that, if your beneficiaries receive an insurance payout, they can invest it at a reasonable rate of interest and get enough income so it fills the gap between their cash needs and any other financial resources they have.

The first thing you need to know, then, is what resources will be available to a surviving spouse. You need to make an accurate assessment of your assets and liabilities, as well as the amount of income that will be needed to cover living expenses. Some questions to think about:

- Does your spouse work?
- Are you burdened with a lot of debts?
- Do you want your children to go to state colleges or private schools?
- Do you want your survivors to live off the income that can be produced from the proceeds from your life insurance, or is it OK for them to invade the principal? (Remember, if they can preserve the principal, they will always have money coming in.)
- Are you covered by group life insurance on the job? If so, how much?
- Do you qualify for Social Security benefits? A surviving spouse who is not yet 60 is eligible for benefits only if she or he is caring for young children—those under 18, or 19 if they are still in high school.

You already know what assets and liabilities you have. You have a pretty good idea of your annual living expenses. Think hard about your income objective. What other sources of income—the salary of the spouse who survives, Social Security benefits, investment income from income-earning assets—will be available to help reduce the gap that insurance needs to fill if the salary of one of you (or of the principal breadwinner) is stopped by death? Divide the gap, or shortfall, by a reasonable rate of interest that you could expect to net on your savings, after taxes.

EXAMPLE: If your gap between what's coming in and what's going out is $7,000 a year, and assuming an after-tax interest rate of 6 percent, you would need $116,667 of life insurance (i.e., $7,000 divided by .06). If you want to take inflation into account, use an even lower rate of return. That will mean you must buy significantly more insurance.

Don't forget other expenses—the funeral, the unreimbursed medical costs of final illness, inheritance taxes, mortgage balance and other debts, and especially an education fund. Put the mortgage balance on this list only if the total balance is expected to be paid off if you die. The alternative is to include continuing mortgage payments as part of the income objective. TIP: Mortgage interest is tax deductible. As a tax benefit, and especially if your mortgage is at a low rate of interest, it may be best to let it continue—if you can plan the financial resources to continue the monthly payments.

Total these other final expenses and add them to the other insurance needs to get a preliminary figure on what you need from insurance.

Next, list the lump-sum benefits that will be available to your family if you die—the proceeds from both group and individual life insurance policies, and any lump-sum pension or profit sharing that is to come to your estate. Subtract these from the preliminary figure you already arrived at, and you will come up with the total amount of life insurance you need.

What Kind of Life Insurance?

Once you know how much life insurance you need, the next question is what kind to buy. Your decision on the type of policy that is best will be based on your need, your age, and how much you can afford to pay—all of which will change over time. The types to consider are:

1. TERM

When you are young, term has the lowest cost of all life insurance. You can buy a large amount at low cost for you and your spouse. The rates will depend to some extent on your state of health and smoking habits. But term provides a death benefit and that is all. The coverage is for a specific length of time, and the death benefit will be paid only if you die during that time. It is basic, economical coverage.

Most term policies are *annual renewable term*. This means the policy is renewed each year, and the premium goes up each year because the probability of death has increased slightly (you are a year older)—regardless of any changes in your health or your occupation or life-style. Until you reach 40, the annual increase in the premium is slight. It goes up more quickly after that.

You can, however, buy *5-, 10-, or 15-year term*. In those policies, the premium stays the same for the length of the term, rises when you renew, and then again stays level until the next renewal.

Decreasing term is an alternative. Your premium cost stays level but your coverage declines. If you buy mortgage insurance, or other debt insurance, decreasing term is what you are getting.

WARNING: Try to avoid a term policy that includes a "reentry" rule. It requires you to requalify some time in the future, maybe 10 or 20 years down the road, by passing a physical examination at that time. If you do not pass, you will then pay extra to continue the coverage. Not all policies require this.

TIP: When you buy term insurance, make sure it can be converted later to a *whole life policy* without your having to take a new physical. This will be a valuable advantage if you have developed any serious illness by the time you want to convert to whole life.

IT-CAN-HAPPEN EXAMPLE: In his late thirties, John bought policies for several hundred thousand dollars' worth of term insurance—an inexpensive buy at his age. A year later, a malignant tumor was removed from his leg. Because the policies were convertible without a new medical exam, he was able to convert them to whole life. Understanding his situation, he budgeted for the higher premiums. When he died at 52, and after his illness had depleted most of his other assets, the policies provided a safety net for his widow.

EXTRA TIP: Be sure you know exactly how long you have the option of converting. And before you convert, check on the cost of a similar policy with another company or two (that is, if you do not anticipate having any trouble passing a physical at a different company).

2. WHOLE LIFE

This is also known as *straight life* or *traditional life* insurance. It covers you as long as you live and pay the premiums. The cost stays the same each year. It is based on your age at the time when you buy the policy and, based on your life expectancy, the premiums are averaged out in advance. As a result, whole life will cost you more than term each year when you are young, but it will be cheaper than term as you get older.

Unlike term, whole life provides more than just the death benefit. It also creates savings, or cash values, and, in some cases, dividends. When you pay each premium, the company uses part to cover the death benefit, part to build cash value, and part to pay for administrative costs and commissions to the salespeople or brokers who sold you the policy.

Cash value builds up over the years of the policy. The company guarantees it at a fixed rate, and its earnings are tax deferred. You can borrow the cash value at a low interest rate specified in your policy and pay it back if and when you want, but remember: The amount you borrowed will be deducted from the death benefit if you die before you have paid it back.

How about dividends? You get them if yours is a *participating whole life policy* with a mutual insurance company. The dividend is really a refund of a premium you paid previously. It depends on the company's investment income, expenses, and the mortality rate of policyholders, so it is not guaranteed. If income is high and expenses and mortality are low, you get a higher dividend.

You get choices about how you take the dividends. You may take them in tax-free cash or leave them to accumulate interest; you may use them to pay premiums or to buy paid-up additions—small amounts of insurance that increase the cash value and raise the death benefit above the original amount.

3. UNIVERSAL LIFE

This is also called *flexible adjustable life*. The company puts your premium into a cash-value account, then each month deducts from it the cost of death benefit and expenses. The part that goes toward the death benefit is about equal to term insurance. The part that stays in your cash-value account accumulates interest on a tax-deferred basis. The amount in your cash-value account is thus "interest-sensitive"—meaning that it can go up or down depending on the financial climate. So altogether, the cash value reflects the premiums you have paid, as well as market conditions.

You can borrow against the cash value, or make partial withdrawals from it, without losing the death benefit. As in whole life, of course, any amount you have borrowed and not paid back will be deducted from the death benefit if you die.

Universal life has a certain flexibility. You may vary the premiums according to your current situation: When you have extra money, you may pay ahead, and, if you are short of funds, you may skip a premium and allow your cash-value account to pay it. WARNING: If you skip too many, you can empty your cash-value account, making your policy lapse or become worthless.

The premiums on universal life cost less than the premiums on whole life. Here's why. Rather than pay dividends, the insurance company increases the interest rate paid on your cash-value account, or cuts the monthly premium on your policy. By controlling the interest rates and guaranteeing a relatively low return (usually 4 to 4.5 percent), the company transfers its investment risk to you, the policyholder.

In view of the uncertainties of the financial markets, you may not think universal life is the better choice. You may prefer the guaranteed rate of interest and inflexible premium of whole life to the flexibility of universal.

4. VARIABLE LIFE

If you are willing to take more risk, this type of policy may be for you. It has universal life's feature: flexible premiums. But your cash-value account is invested in the securities market, usually in mutual funds. The death benefit then goes up or down with the market, but not below a certain stated minimum. If the stock market drops severely, the company may ask you to pay extra to keep your insurance in force.

Variable life is regulated by the Securities and Exchange Commission. The law requires that you be sent a prospectus before buying a policy.

Features of Cash-Value Accounts

One of the most valuable features of a cash-value policy is that you can use the accumulated savings to help pay for a college education or to supplement your retirement income. Another important consideration, especially in view of your plan to retire or change careers at a young age: You can decide to stop paying the premiums after the policy has been in force for a certain number of years (how many depends on the terms of your particular policy). Your policy will tell you the minimum cash value that will be available at the end of any year. You can then turn your insurance to your advantage by using one of several options:

• Cash in the policy and invest the cash value as you see fit. This means, of course, that you no longer have the coverage, which is fine *if you no longer need the coverage.* Perhaps, for example, you bought the policy to provide a certain death benefit for your family while your children were young, knowing that the cash value would be available for you to use when they were grown and on their own.

• Ask the company to use the cash value to provide you with *extended term insurance*—in effect, a term policy. The company will continue the same death benefits (less any outstanding loans at the time when you die) for a specific length of time that is stated in your policy. You pay no more premiums.

• Use the cash value to buy a *paid-up policy.* It will have a smaller face value than your present policy, but you will have continued coverage without paying any more premiums. This will reduce your fixed expenses by eliminating that annual premium—important if you need the coverage but are cutting down expenses.

WARNING: Do not commit funds that you will need in the near future to a cash-value life insurance policy. To discourage you from cashing in your policy early, the company will charge you a "surrender fee." In the first five to seven years of the policy, it will be substantial.

Think of the cash-value account as long-term savings, but certainly not as your only form of saving. And be wary of insurance salespeople who sell these policies as investment vehicles, putting the emphasis on their growth aspect because they are tax-deferred. The primary purpose of life insurance is to replace future income that would be lost if you died prematurely. Saving taxes is not the purpose, so don't confuse that with insurance on your life. If you are young, need maximum protection, and have a tight cash flow, tax deferral is a very poor reason for buying cash-value life insurance.

Nor should you let yourself be sold on a policy that leaves you underinsured. Too many young people are sold policies they can't *afford*, at cash-value rates, rather than policies they *need*, at term rates. If the amount you can afford to pay from the family budget will not buy adequate insurance in a cash-value policy, but it will buy adequate insurance in a term policy, your choice should be obvious: Buy the coverage you need.

If you can afford the premiums on a cash-value policy, and if it is providing the insurance coverage you need, the cash value that builds up over the years will provide an excellent base for funding the education of your children or for your own retirement income. Some people, however, suggest you "buy term and invest the rest." That is, if you can afford whole life, you buy only term and invest the difference between its cost and what you would have to pay for whole life. Think about that. It forces you to face some tough questions: Can you discipline yourself to invest that difference, year in, year out? How about your ability to select investments that will earn what you need over the next 10 to 20 years—do you trust that ability? Are you sure you will not touch your investment—will not *have* to touch your investment—until you need it at, say, age 50 or 55?

At least once a year, take a good look at your insurance policies and your insurance needs. Has your family changed? Any new births? Any college graduates out and earning their own way? Any other responsibilities added or subtracted? Do your homework, consult a reliable agent, figure out your needs, and you will be comfortable in making insurance decisions.

Disability Insurance

Nobody wants to think about being disabled. But people do become disabled, through accident or illness, temporarily and permanently. The only protection you have from losing your income, with disastrous results for the family budget, is disability insurance. To make yourself think seriously about it, consider these questions:

- If an accident or illness kept you from working all next year, how would you replace your spendable income?
- Who would pay the rent or mortgage, the car payments, the other monthly fixed expenses—not to mention the day-to-day, out-of-pocket costs?
- Could your family adjust financially to losing your income, or your spouse's?
- Where would such a catastrophe leave your dream of early retirement?
- How would you cover the cost of home care, unreimbursed medical expenses, or hiring someone to do the around-the-house jobs that you usually do?

The fact is, diseases that once were killers are now disablers. The skills of medical science have changed the effects of heart disease, hypertension, strokes, breast cancer (and many other types of cancer), and countless other serious physical ailments, making them much more likely to disable than kill. Insurance underwriters study the statistics and announce that if you are between 35 and 65 years old, you are three or four times as likely to be disabled for at least 90 days as you are to die during those years. That is sobering news.

Disability insurance protects against the loss of your most valuable asset—your ability to earn money. Because it protects against loss of income, it is available only to people who are employed. Many employers today provide disability insurance among the other fringe benefits, usually in a group policy. Often it is a short-term policy, paying benefits for only two years or so, and usually it replaces only a fixed percentage of your salary, up to a maximum—but not your total gross pay. Your total, remember, may include bonuses, commissions, tips, incentive plans, contributions to your pension, and partnership distributions. Paradoxically, the higher your salary, the lower the percentage of replacement—in most cases. If you face that paradox, you will be smart to buy an individual disability policy.

If you happen to become disabled before you reach 65, Social Security can help. It will start paying you disability benefits if you have a physical or mental condition so severe that it prevents you from working and is expected to last at least 12 months, or if it is expected to result in death. But it is stringent: Almost three-quarters of the disability claims filed with Social Security are rejected.

If you are considering buying an individual disability policy to supplement the group policy where you work, or because you have no group policy at work, think about these questions:

1. *Can the policy be canceled by the insurance company?* You want to be sure it cannot be canceled before the end of the contract period, as long as you pay the premiums on time.

2. *Is the policy guaranteed renewable?* Make sure you have the right to renew it on the same terms and at the same rate until you reach 65. Even if you change jobs or careers or become unemployed, or take a cut in pay, you have a right to the same coverage you bought at the outset.

3. *What is the definition of "disability" in the particular policy you are buying?* The standard definition is that you are disabled if you are under a doctor's care and unable to perform important duties of your job. But after that basic definition come some differences.

Some policies pay only if you are unable to perform any work at all. Others cover you as long as you are suffering a loss of income, even if you are working in another job. Still others cover you in your specific job, regardless of any other income you may be getting.

These policies—more expensive than the usual ones—will pay you benefits if you return to work but at a lower paying job that is not your usual, or previous, occupation. They are known in the business as "own occ" policies. For example, a surgeon who suffers from a disability that prevents him or her from continuing to perform surgery, but who is able to work in the emergency room at substantially lower pay, will get full benefits if the policy is "own occ."

An alternative to "own occ" is the "any occ" or "any occupation" policy—also known as an *income replacement policy.* It covers you whether you are able to work full-time, part-time, or not at all. It simply replaces a percentage of the income you are losing because of your disability. Some policies, you will find, provide "own occ" for the first couple of years of a disability, then "any occ" thereafter. Check out what you are being offered before you sign up.

4. *How long is the elimination period?* This is the length of time you must be disabled before the insurance company starts paying benefits. The shorter the waiting period, the more you pay for the policy. The period may be 30, 60, 90, 180, or 360 days.

If you have put away enough emergency funds (equal to at least six months' regular pay, remember? and more is better), or if your company's group disability policy kicks in after a very short waiting period, you can get a much lower premium by buying a policy with a long elimination period. WARNING: Your first check will not arrive until one month *after* the end of the waiting period. If your policy's elimination period is 180 days, your first check will arrive after 210 days.

5. *What about partial or residual benefits?* In most policies, if your income is diminished by a certain percentage (usually at least 20 percent), you will get that percentage of your benefits for as long as you are disabled. Some policies will pay your full benefits—100 percent—if you have lost more than 75 or 80 percent of your income. Some policies require you to be fully disabled before you can receive residual benefits; others do not.

6. *Does the policy cover pregnancy and maternity?* Some cover only medical complications due to pregnancy. Others cover any normal pregnancy, but set a 90-day waiting period regardless of the length of the waiting period for other disabilities.

7. *How long will the policy continue to pay benefits?* Check this one carefully. Some policies cover only a specified number of years (maybe 5 or 10), some go to age 65 and stop, some are for your lifetime. You must figure out which one makes the most sense in *your* situation. For instance, if you have assets set aside for retirement, and income from them, plus Social Security, you need to insure yourself only to age 65. If you are young and don't have much in savings, if you have no pension plan, if you don't have enough quarters of earnings recorded with Social Security to qualify for disability or retirement benefits—ask yourself if you could afford to live to the age of 65 or beyond if you were disabled.

8. *Is there a future-income option?* With this option, you can buy greater coverage as your income increases, without having to take another physical exam. You will, however, have to pay a premium that matches your age at the time of each increase.

9. *Are the disability benefits taxable?* If you become disabled and claim benefits on a policy that your employer pays for, you must pay income tax on the amount you get. If you have been paying the premiums yourself, the benefits are not taxable.

The Best: A Coordinated Plan

The ideal way to protect yourself against disability is to coordinate an individual insurance policy with group coverage, so your own policy picks up where your company policy leaves off. When you leave your company, of course, you leave the group policy behind.

How much do you pay for disability insurance? Your premium depends on your age, occupation, and medical history. The insurance company will contact your doctors and check your medical records. It will ask for samples of your blood and urine and, depending on the amount of coverage you are applying for, an electrocardiogram, AIDS test, cholesterol count, diabetes test, and histories of drug and tobacco use. The policy the company writes may then stipulate that it will not cover you for a preexisting condition. If you have a "bad back," for example, the policy may state that problems with your back will not qualify you for disability benefits.

An important advantage of an individual policy is that, if it is noncancelable and guaranteed renewable, it will remain in force as long as you pay the premiums. If you change jobs or careers, or become unemployed, you may be awfully glad you have it.

EXAMPLE: John, whose illness started with the leg tumor, had no individual disability policy, but had some fringe benefits on his job. After exhausting them, he had to start going into his and his wife's assets. By the time he died, there was almost nothing left for her other than the money from his whole life insurance policies—the ones he had been able to convert from term when his illness was diagnosed. His widow is an avid proponent of individual disability protection.

CHAPTER 15

Estate Planning

You have been saving to meet your primary goal—early retirement—by taking advantage of tax-sheltered plans at work and by making other investments. You have been creating and accumulating wealth. How do you protect that wealth so you can pass some (if not all) of it on to those you love who survive you?

The answer is *estate planning*—planning what is to become of everything you own, and conserving as much of your assets as possible and transferring them to your heirs in the way you want at the lowest possible cost in taxes. By reading this book, you have put yourself on the road to estate planning. You know your assets and liabilities. You know who owns what. You understand your income and expenses, how much life insurance you have or need, how much you can look forward to in retirement benefits.

Think of estate planning as a three-part process: (1) drawing up a will, (2) establishing testamentary or living trusts, and (3) minimizing federal estate taxes. Yet, in a sense, it is one process, for your will and estate plan are done at the same time. Simultaneously, you plan for the needs of your spouse and family and take advantage of the many ways in which you can reduce or avoid taxes and other expenses that can shrink your estate.

Your Will

To make sure that your estate gets into the hands of those you intend it for, you need a will. Your will states how you want your property handled after your death. It names guardians for any children you have who are still minors. If you die without a will, the law in the state where you live will determine what happens to your assets. And the state will name a guardian for your children. Under the law, whether your heirs like it or not, your assets and your children can go not where you want but where the state wants.

WARNING: Some people say, "Oh, I don't need a will. Everything I have is jointly owned. And I've named beneficiaries for all my retirement accounts." That attitude invites tremendous problems when it comes down to estate taxes. If your estate totals less than $600,000, it escapes federal estate tax. But it is quite likely that, as you build up your corporate benefits (e.g., 401(k), IRAs, pension and profit-sharing plans, retirement stock) and add in your primary residence, vacation home, insurance benefits (including group, don't forget), and other investments, you will arrive at a taxable estate that goes over $600,000. The tax bite can be big—anywhere from 37 to 55 percent of your taxable estate.

You *are* allowed to leave your entire estate to your spouse without paying any tax. This is called the *unlimited marital deduction.* But the government will collect after your spouse dies. And all that jointly held property and retirement benefits, added to a surviving spouses's own assets, may swell his or her estate to too large a size—in which case, the Feds have a hand out, ready to take theirs. Careful planning while you are both alive can minimize estate taxes.

Your will is a formal legal document. In most states, you must execute it in writing and sign it in the presence of two witnesses who also sign in your presence. (If necessary, they can later be called into court to testify that they saw you sign that will.)

Your will can specify an executor, who may be a friend or relative or a banker or lawyer (or bank or law firm—remember that it will be many years, you hope, before your will is put to use). The executor will be responsible for taking your will through probate and making sure that your estate is disposed of as you intended, so think about that. You need to name someone who is both willing and able to handle the process, which can be time-consuming.

As for the guardian or guardians for your minor children, be sure to talk it over with the person you plan to name. If the guardian lacks financial know-how, but would be well qualified in terms of making a home for your children and seeing that they are taken care of as you want them to be, you can name someone else to handle the kids' financial affairs. The important thing is to be candid and establish mutual confidence with the proposed guardian.

What do you say in your will? You decide who is to get what from your estate, and say so in plain good English. WARNING: Be careful with specific bequests. If you want to leave Auntie's teapot and a number of such items of sentimental value to a number of specific people, make a separate list of all of them and give the list to the executor or other trusted person to distribute. Otherwise, if they are listed in your will, you will have to make a change in your will every time you dispose of one of the items or the person who is supposed to get one dies before you do—an expensive way to handle distribution, as you pay for a trip through your lawyer's office each time.

EXCEPTION: If you own an extensive coin collection or a priceless work of art, for example, you will want to make a specific bequest.

If you and your spouse hold property jointly, it passes directly to the survivor when either of you dies. It is not passed on by the will and does not go through probate. Nor do proceeds from life insurance (nor group life insurance) and your retirement benefits, since you have named a beneficiary. IMPORTANT: Remember, however, that for tax purposes half of the value of all such property is counted as part of your gross estate.

Trusts

Trusts can be used to minimize your estate taxes, avoid probate, and manage your assets. A trust is a good way to protect children of a previous marriage. What is a trust? It is a legal arrangement in which control over property is transferred from you to a person or organization (the *trustee*) for the benefit of someone else (the *beneficiary*). As the person setting up the trust, you are the *grantor*. And, as the grantor, you may make yourself the trustee.

Think of two kinds of trusts: *inter vivos*, or living, and testamentary. A living trust goes into effect while you, the grantor, are alive. A testamentary trust is established by your will and does not take effect until you die.

1. Living Trust

You can make a living trust either revocable (i.e., you have total control over the assets in the trust) or irrevocable (i.e., you give up control over the assets). The assets in a revocable living trust will eventually be included in your estate, but in the meantime a living trust can give you an orderly way to manage such assets. This is ideal if you are off globe-trotting or if you simply do not want to manage your own assets. Meanwhile, you keep total control. You pay taxes on any earnings. You may withdraw some of the principal. On your death, the assets are not subject to probate because the owner of the assets was not you—the legal owner was the trust.

For all this to happen, you must change the title to your assets so the trust has title. This will cost you some legal fees; it can be an expensive nuisance. Since you will continue to accumulate assets, you will still need a will. It must provide that any property you own will "pour over" into the trust when you die.

WARNING: If you yourself are the trustee, it is important to name a successor trustee to take over if you should become incapacitated and unable to handle your financial affairs. If you do this, the trust can work quite well.

If you establish an irrevocable living trust, you minimize estate taxes. But you give up control over assets that you might need in the future. WARNING: Once you put something into an irrevocable trust, you cannot get it back.

An alternative to a living trust is a *power of attorney*. Suppose you are going off on a trip around the world for six months. You want to see that your bills are paid while you are gone. You give a family member (or anyone else whom you trust) a specific power of attorney over your checking and savings accounts. That person can then sign your checks and transfer your money between accounts. And you can fly or sail carefree.

A *durable power of attorney* anticipates a more serious situation: the possibility that you may become incapacitated. The durable power of attorney enables the person you have named to take over all your financial affairs if you are unable to handle them. If such a situation arises, and if you have not signed a durable power of attorney or named a successor trustee to a living trust, your family might have to go to court to get a guardian appointed to manage your affairs.

2. Testamentary Trust

The advantage of this trust is that you are assured that your assets will be managed after your death in the way you want them to be. Your will establishes the trust (or trusts), and nothing takes effect until you die.

The most valuable types of testamentary trusts are those that help you to avoid or minimize estate taxes:

1. BYPASS TRUST

This is also known as a *unified credit shelter trust*. As already discussed, the unlimited marital deduction under federal estate tax law lets you leave your entire estate to your spouse without paying any tax. But when your spouse dies, any amount above $600,000 in his or her estate will be taxed. For instance, an estate of $700,000 must pay $37,000 (i.e., a whopping 37 percent) in federal estate taxes.

How to avoid this big bite? Suppose your estate is $1.2 million. One way to minimize the tax is to divide your estate into two parts. Put $600,000 into a bypass, or unified credit shelter, trust. Put the other $600,000 into a marital trust, or give it outright to your spouse. Upon your spouse's death, the assets in the bypass trust will go to your children (or to any other beneficiary you name), and in the meantime your spouse may receive income, or even take part of the principal, during her or his lifetime. The balance of the estate (i.e., the second $600,000, or more if the balance has risen above that), will go to your surviving spouse through the marital trust—if you have not previously given it outright. At his or her death, that second $600,000 will pass on to heirs without federal estate taxes. If that second $600,000 has grown larger, of course, the amount over $600,000 will be taxed.

Some added points to remember:

- The bypass trust can be used only by setting it up in your will.
- It must be written into both spouse's wills, and is utilized by the estate of the first to die.
- All assets that go into your bypass trust must be owned only by you; you are not allowed to put jointly held property into a bypass trust. TIP: This is a good reason for young married couples to begin estate planning with separate ownership of some property, such as investments.
- EXTRA TIP: To equalize the estates of both spouses, you may want to transfer some assets to the "poorer" of the two.

But what if your estate will be less than $1.2 million, but well over $600,000? And what if you cannot transfer assets to your spouse during your lifetime—assets in your name only, such as retirement benefits and group life insurance. In other words, maybe there are not enough liquid assets to transfer to the "poorer" spouse. Or maybe you both have few assets right now but expect them to grow in years to come, and you don't want to keep redrawing your wills.

One solution: In each of your wills, include a disclaimer that says you choose not to inherit all or part of your spouse's assets. Those that a spouse disclaims can go into a bypass trust, so they will not be a part of his or her estate upon death. In this case, the spouse would disclaim $600,000, and would receive any remaining assets outright.

As you save more and more each year for retirement, you increase the value of your estate. At the same time, when you buy more insurance or your group life insurance is increased (probably automatically with each raise in your pay), your estate goes up. Before you know it, you can have an estate-planning problem. The disclaimer can work until your assets get to the $1.2 million mark. Then consider setting up a bypass trust in your will.

2. QTIP TRUST

Suppose you want your spouse to have a life interest in a trust and receive income from it, but you want to keep control over who will inherit the property after your spouse's death. This may be the situation, for instance, in a second marriage, where you want to provide for your present spouse while you conserve assets for the benefit of children from a previous marriage. What you do is establish a *Qualified Terminable Interest Property (QTIP)* trust. It holds onto property that would otherwise go outright to a spouse or would be put into a marital trust.

3. IRREVOCABLE LIFE INSURANCE TRUST

Life insurance seems to have special rules: Your beneficiary can receive the proceeds from your policy without paying any federal income tax, but, when federal estate taxes are calculated, life insurance money is included in the estate. A substantial policy can raise an estate above the $600,000 line. One way to get life insurance out of your taxable estate is to establish a *life insurance trust*. It must be irrevocable—so you are not permitted to change your mind—and you may not name yourself as trustee.

Here's how it works. The trust owns the life insurance policy. It pays the premiums from funds that you, as grantor, give to the trust.

WARNING: You may transfer all your existing policies to the trust, but don't die within three years after you do that or the benefits from the insurance policies will be included in your estate—just as if the trust never existed. To avoid the three-year rule, set up the trust first, and have it buy a new life insurance policy. The trust buys it in the trust's name. Thus you have never owned the policy.

TIPS:

• Since the trust is irrevocable, list the beneficiary as "my current spouse" or "my spouse at the time of my death" in case a divorce occurs after you create the trust.

• When the insured person dies, the spouse is entitled to receive the income from the trust and to withdraw some of the principal—but there is no law that requires this. If the spouse doesn't need the income or principal, the money in the trust can grow substantially for the benefit of the children or other future heirs, and when it passes to them they will not have to pay any federal estate taxes on it.

• Look for a new kind of life insurance called "second-to-die." It is being bought by many life insurance trusts. The policy is issued on the lives of both spouses. The premium, based on two lives, is lower than if you bought two individual policies. A "second-to-die" policy pays off only when the second of the two spouses dies, when estate taxes are due. Because the proceeds, which are paid in cash, are not included in the estate, they can then help pay the estate taxes. Without that cash, an estate might have to liquidate assets to pay Uncle Sam.

• If you are single and expect to have an estate worth more than $600,000, a life insurance trust can be used to pay the estate tax. Otherwise, if the taxes are paid out of your estate, your family members, children from a previous marriage, or others to whom you are leaving bequests will get less than you planned. You set this up by "gifting" money to the trust to pay the insurance premiums—in effect, prepaying part of the future estate taxes (the premiums could be lower than the amount of taxes that will be due when you die). If you are divorced and single, you might ask your adult children to buy an insurance policy on your life. They own the policy. You pay the premiums. This can save you the cost of setting up a life insurance trust, yet the policy will ultimately provide the cash to pay your estate taxes. WARNING: You may think of transferring a life insurance policy you already own to a trust held by your children, and "gifting" them the money to pay the premiums. This is complex, and may be subject to a gift tax, so get good legal advice before you establish such an irrevocable life insurance trust.

NOTE: You may give as much as $10,000 a year to each of as many people as you want to without having to file a gift-tax return. Your spouse may do the same—so the total allowed as a married couple is $20,000 annually. Whomever you give it to gets the money free of income taxes.

Don't forget that it is not only the federal government that taxes your estate. So does every state except Nevada. But some states set lower rates than others, and usually the tax depends on who the heirs are and how much they will get. So check out the law in your state or in any state you are thinking about moving to.

WARNING: If you have homes in more than one state, make sure it is quite clear which one is your permanent residence. If this is not clear, your heirs could find more than one state trying to get a bite out of your estate, with each state where you own property insisting on probate. Be sure you vote, register your car and driver's license, and have clear title to a home in the state that gives you the best tax advantage. If you are contemplating a move to another state, find a knowledgeable lawyer who can analyze your situation and make recommendations.

Lawyers, in fact, are indispensable to estate planning. Do-it-yourselfing in this area will probably cost your heirs more in estate taxes than you would have paid for expert advice. Setting up trusts and writing a "bulletproof" will is best left to attorneys who specialize in the field.

CHAPTER 16

Record Keeping

How's your home filing system?

Got a couple of four-drawer filing cabinets filled with file folders—everything marked in A to Z order? With subfiles under major headings, like an office?

If not, you are not alone. Most people are just not that buttoned up. Nor do they—or *you*—need to be. But you *do* need to have some kind of logical system of keeping your records where (a) someone else can find them, and (b) if someone else finds them, that someone can make sense out of them.

Maybe you have piles of papers, bank statements, pension booklets, tax records from earlier years, sitting in a box or piled up all over your desk or the floor. If you do, it is time to set up a simple home filing system—a practical system that keeps track of your financial matters and important papers related to them over a long time.

Filing away financial papers is not fun. But not having them filed so you can retrieve them easily when you have to is a costly mistake. Accurate records can help you cut taxes by reminding you of deductible items. They can help you weed out poor investments. They can help your heirs unscramble any number of problems after you are gone.

Probably you have known more than one newly widowed woman who was at a loss to find her husband's life insurance policies or lists of investments, a situation guaranteed to turn grief into anger.

Any banker can tell you about unclaimed accounts. Banks regularly take out local newspaper advertisements listing the names and last known addresses of countless customers who have left their bank accounts inactive for so long they've forgotten about them, or their heirs have been unaware of them. If a bank cannot locate the owner of an account, the unclaimed money goes, after a certain period, to the state. In fact, state treasuries hold millions of dollars from bank accounts, stock dividends, utility deposits, and insurance settlements simply because no one can trace the assets to their rightful owners. Of the total, only about 25 percent ever gets recovered by the rightful owners or their heirs. The grand total of unclaimed money in the U.S. is close to $1 billion.

Imagine what would happen if you were named executor of your parents' or grandparents' estates—and if you lived thousands of miles away and had no idea of just what assets or life insurance policies they had. Then imagine your sense of relief if you found a notebook that listed all of their savings and investments, told you where to find all of their important documents, and added the names of their lawyer, stockbroker, or others who had advised them. Not only would your life be easier, but that notebook would probably save the estate some money.

Think also about what you have to go through to replace missing records. Getting your state's motor vehicle department to replace a certificate of title for your car can take forever—a period during which the good price you've been offered may give up and go away. If you want to replace a lost stock certificate, the company will insist that you sign a witnessed affidavit that the certificate was lost or destroyed and they will want you to put up a surety bond. That can cost you as much as 3 percent of the current market price of the stock.

Your Safe Deposit Box

Certificates of title, stock certificates—such hard-to-replace items should be kept in a safe deposit box. What else to put in the box? Any and all of the following:

Birth certificates
Stock certificates
Marriage certificate
Citizenship papers
Bonds
Certificates of title (automobile, truck, motorcycle)
Real estate deeds
Copies of wills (but not the signed originals)
Divorce decree
Death certificates
Passports
Discharge papers from military service
Veterans Administration papers
Adoption papers
Contracts
Household inventory (with photographs, for appraisal purposes)

WARNING: When either one of the owners of a safe deposit box dies, the bank seals the box until all tax and legal matters are taken care of. It will grant access only when it gets legal permission; the box may then be opened only in the presence of a legally authorized person, usually a bank officer. That is why it is important *not* to keep the signed originals of your wills in your safe deposit box. Rather, have your lawyer keep them in the firm's vault. And keep life insurance policies at home, so that proceeds from them can be claimed quickly if they are needed. (Often, life insurance benefits are the only money a new widow has to live on until an estate is settled.)

A four-drawer steel filing cabinet is nice. But it is not essential. Corrugated cardboard boxes will do just fine. An ideal size is the sturdy carton in which supermarkets receive 12 32-ounce bottles of soft drinks. It is perfect for holding letter-size file folders (9¼ × 11¾ inches) and has convenient handholds punched through at each end. It lasts for years.

Into your files go all the papers that keep you—and, if necessary, others—up to date on your assets and liabilities and the identities of those who will be helpful if you die or become disabled. "Up to date" is important. Go through your files regularly (at least once a year) and throw out whatever is no longer needed. You certainly don't need to keep an insurance policy on a car you junked five years ago.

What to File, What to Keep, What to Toss

Following are a variety of tips on how to file, what to file, and how long to keep certain files:

• *File folders and notebooks.* These are important. They keep you organized. Label each folder or notebook clearly so you know at a glance what is inside. The notebook is a good way to track your stocks, bonds, and mutual funds, so you can see when you bought a particular investment, and what you paid for it. File statements from mutual funds or stockbrokers so the most recent is at the front (or on top) of the file. REMEMBER: If the mutual fund is not in a retirement account, you will need to keep track of dividends and interest that you either received or reinvested. You paid taxes on them, which in turn affects the cost basis of the fund (see chapter 11).

Be sure all your statements from Individual Retirement Accounts (IRAs) go into your looseleaf binder. This is especially important if you have made contributions that are *nondeductible* because, if you do not have verification, you could end up paying taxes on withdrawals from those nondeductible accounts. (The money you have put into them, remember, is money on which you had already paid withholding taxes.)

• *Tax returns.* Keep all your Internal Revenue Service (IRS) returns. They may come in handy for years to come. But weed out from your files after three years all the backup material you assembled in order to prepare your tax return. The IRS may not go back earlier than three years to audit you—unless they are out to prove a fraud or gross negligence.

• *Canceled checks.* Like IRS returns, keep for three years—except those that paid for home improvements.

• *Home improvements.* Keep records of payments, and canceled checks, for all home improvements until you sell the house. At that time, it will be important to be able to prove how much you have put into the house, since you will be taxed on the gain between what the house cost you (i.e., original purchase price *plus* improvements) and what you sell it for. Did you add a deck or a family room, remodel the kitchen, convert a garage, plant shrubs and trees, put extra insulation in the attic, or install energy-saving devices? All are permanent home improvements.

• *Bills paid.* Keep a continuing file over each year, to help when you prepare your income-tax return. Then sort, and toss all except those that substantiate tax deductions and home improvements. Your "bills paid" file will also be invaluable when you review your spending plan for last year and set up your plan for next year.

In addition to these specific files, you should keep all of the following, each in its labeled file folder:

Advisers (list of, with addresses and phone numbers)
Annuities
Bankbooks and statements
Children's records (including education record of each)
Credit histories
Employment history
Gift tax returns
Gifts
Inheritances
Insurance policies and records of claims, etc.
   Auto
   Disability
   Health (i.e., medical)
   Homeowner's
   Life
   Medicare (file separately from other health insurance)

Loans (applications for and records of)
Property taxes (bills and receipts)
Real estate investments
Retirement
  401(k) plan
  IRA (individual retirement account)
  Keogh plan
  Money-market funds
  Mutual funds
  Pension plan
  Profit-sharing plan
Social Security
  Earnings records
  Numbers
State income-tax returns
Stock options
Warranties and guarantees
Wills (file signed original with your lawyer)

If your record system has been nonexistent or catch-as-catch-can, take a weekend now to set up a practical, working system. Setting up, let's face it, is real work. No fun. But once you have done it, you will be thrilled the first time you go looking for a particular piece of information and find it is actually where you thought it would be. You will never find a better remedy than that for an anxiety attack brought on, perhaps, by your accountant asking for some important piece of financial information.

Then, file regularly. As you receive reports, pay bills, or send off claims, file promptly. If you cannot file promptly, maintain a "to file" box, and put everything that you *should* be filing into it. Then, every couple of months, force yourself to do the real filing. If you are married, do it together or take turns. Don't let it pile up. Procrastination begets chaos.

TIP: Always keep files accessible. If you stash them in the basement or attic, where they are hard to get to, you will defeat your purpose.

CHAPTER 17

Putting It All Together

Real-Life Scenarios for Kissing the Rat Race Good-bye

You've learned and absorbed a lot of information about doing hard-nosed financial planning toward your goal of financial independence in 10 to 15 years. At this point, you may be wondering just how possible it really is for you to accumulate the money you need to kiss the rat race good-bye by the time you are 45 or 50.

To build your confidence, we'll first take a look at three examples of how it's been or is being done—two are couples, one on a pension and one without a pension, and the third is a 35-year-old single woman. What you'll see clearly is that they have all applied the advice that is the cornerstone on which this book is built—start to plan early and save, save, save.

Then we'll take a look at building a second career in a little more detail because that is probably one of the chief reasons many are thinking of breaking out of the corporate routine—to pursue a dream on their own terms without reporting to anyone but themselves. Then, if you still need more encouragement, keep reading for more suggestions on how you can pull it off.

Howie and Nora: Early Planning, Committed Saving, and Sound Investing

Howie was a manufacturer's rep, selling handbags and costume jewelry to stores. But, as an independent salesman, he never built up any corporate pension benefits. Nor did Nora, who was an able legal secretary. They bought their house in 1968 for $50,000, and stayed in it until they "retired" at age 48 in 1986. They sold the house for $275,000, and were able to pay off their small mortgage (about $37,000 at that point), buy a condo, and pay off the realtor's commission and legal fees. The condo is worth less today, as they are well aware, but they agree that they are not about to move.

As a salesman Howie had done so much traveling during the week that all he wanted to do was relax near home on weekends and vacations. Soon after they moved into the house they bought a boat that they could live on over weekends and vacations. By keeping the boat in good shape, they were able to sell it for about $60,000 when they sold the house.

It was save, save, save all during their married life, and especially in the 14 years before they retired. Total savings were usually anywhere from 7 to 15 percent of their pay, every year. Since Howie's income could (and did!) vary widely from year to year, the percentage was sometimes lower. "When we were first married," he says, "those first couple of years, we saved only about $2,000 a year. Other years, we saw as much as $10,000, even $15,000. There were even a couple of years when I had fantastic sales and we put away $20,000 a year. Not bad."

Howie remembers how closely they worked with their stockbroker. "We took some risks, sure," he says. "We were willing to. But we had some terrific gains. We were always adding to our portfolio and we always let the dividends and interest plow right back in for reinvestment."

By 1986, Howie and Nora had more than half a million dollars in their portfolio. "I could have saved on taxes by opening a Keogh plan," he says, "but I knew I was going to want the money before I got to be 59½. We were reinvesting for growth, for the long haul. Then, when we did retire, we repositioned our investments to give us two things—current income and growth."

Currently, their portfolio gives them about $45,000 a year in income, and the interest and dividends go directly into a money-market account on which Nora and Howie can draw. All gains are reinvested. Expenses? "Minimal," says Nora. "No mortgage. The condo is easier to maintain—and cheaper—than a house."

Nora has signed on with a temp agency, so she works as a secretary only when she wants to. She takes assignments for two- or three-month periods, but the agency knows she is not available during the summer or during winter vacation trips. She earns about $10,000 a year. "I can make as little or as much as I want, that way," she says, "and I'm meeting new people and learning new skills all the time."

Howie takes in from $8,000 to $10,000 a year doing something he has enjoyed since he was a teenager—flying charter trips for a service out of the local airport. "It's good pocket money," he says, "and I get to go places at someone else's expense."

Howie's advice? "Save money. We earned a good living, and now we're enjoying our time. We don't owe anybody anything, and we almost never did have any real debt. Just the mortgage, that was all. I'd tell anybody—if you can't afford it, don't buy it. Don't charge it, whatever it is. When we bought a boat and an airplane, we bought them outright."

Nora adds a thought. "We work when we want and relax when we want. It took discipline to save during our working years but it was worth it—now we're enjoying the money to do whatever we damn well please."

Ken and Shelley: Retired on Two
Pensions *and* Their Own Business

Ken retired when he was 51 after teaching Russian for 26 years in New Jersey public schools. His wife, Shelley, also a teacher, re-tired at the same time and became his business manager, handling the financial and marketing side of the pottery business he had developed since he was given a potter's wheel 15 years earlier.

Without the pottery business thriving and making money, Ken and Shelley could not have retired when they did. For 10 years they had developed his hobby into a profitable business. At the same time, they concentrated on planning for the day when they could both step out of the classroom for good.

By the time they left the classroom, they were grossing about $20,000 a year from selling pottery, mainly at craft fairs. Their expenses ran about $8,000, so they were netting $12,000. Since they had both been with the school system for more than 25 years, their pensions, totaling $32,000 a year, were available immediately. In addition, they get about $4,000 a year in rental income from a house they own jointly with friends—making a gross income of $56,000. That's about 65 percent of the $80,000 they were grossing together when they both worked in the school system.

Shelley was putting money away in an annuity and, during the year before they retired, she saved her entire salary—a good chunk of it went into the annuity and the balance into the bank. They made it a point to live entirely on his income—about $45,000. They gave up a housekeeper, cut out costly meals on the road, and used their camper rather than motels when they made overnight trips to craft fairs. When Shelley left the school system, her annuity had a value of $100,000. It is growing on a tax-deferred basis and she expects there will be at least $200,000 when she is 59½.

With Ken's artistic background and fluency in Russian, he and Shelley spent nine months in Russia with the United States Information Agency (USIA). They made money exchanging dollars for rubles and had expenses paid while they were there, and saved on expenses at home. Luckily, before they retired they got in the habit of watching expenses closely, a valuable habit, they realized, when they returned to find that the U.S. economy was slowing down and moving into recession. Pottery sales at craft fairs were down and so was investment income. Ken had to build up his inventory—it was like starting all over again to get back into the craft fairs. If the pottery business continues to be slow because of the weak economy Shelley is not adverse to taking some money out of the annuity if they need it. As she says, "That's what it is there for and so I'll pay a penalty and taxes."

Two further dividends: the freedom they enjoy, going where they want when they want, and the time they have together.

Judy: Building a Real Estate Investment
to Carry Her to the Islands

Like many in her family, Judy moved to the United States from the Caribbean. By the time she was 28, after working in a bank for several years, she and a friend were able to buy a house together for $105,000. Then she joined a real estate brokerage firm. "Couldn't have been at a worse time, so far as the real estate market is concerned," she says, "but I knew I had to make a change. That corporate environment—that's not for me."

Buying at that "worst time," they signed for a variable-rate mortgage. Payments were $1,000 a month, then increased to $1,200. But Judy and her friend went to work to make the house a gem. They put in new windows and updated the heating system. They created a second-floor apartment that rents for $500 a month.

Even though the value of most houses has dropped since they bought theirs, Judy's house has gone up because of the improvements they have made. It was appraised for $148,000 when they refinanced it in 1991. This time they were able to get a 6 percent rate—a far cry from the 11.5 percent they originally paid. They increased the size of their mortgage to help them buy a car (they also used savings), and wound up with monthly payments at $863— and the apartment rent still coming in to offset a big chunk of their payment.

"This year, I'll make about $60,000 even in this lousy real estate market," said Judy in 1992. "I'm hustling, and I love it, but I can't keep up this pace forever. By the time I'm 50—in about 15 years— I'll quit and go back to the islands. I still have family there."

Judy keeps her needs simple. She splurges, she says, only on clothes and vacations. She carries almost no consumer debt, and saves as much as $12,000 a year. She adds that the 401(k) plan in her office is limited: Employees may put in only $1,500 a year, but

WORKSHEET VIII: FILLING THE GAP:
TOTAL SAVINGS NEEDED

Judy	Age Expected to Retire	Estimated Years in Retirement	Estimated Years to Retirement
Husband	50	30	15
Wife			

Estimated Inflation Rate ___4___

Estimated Rate of Return ___10___

1. Desired Gross Annual Income   35,000
   (Use 70 to 80% of present income)
   Husband _____
   Wife _____

2. Estimated Annual Social Security Benefit
   (Amount you would receive if retiring this year)
   Husband _13,000_
   Wife _____   13,000

3. Estimated Annual Income from Defined Benefit
   Plan(s) at Anticipated Retirement Date
     Husband 1 _____   2 _____   _____
     Wife   1 _____   2 _____   _____

4. Inflation Adjustment Factor—Table 8
   (Inflation Adjustment for Pension without COLA)
     Husband _____
     Wife _____

5. Inflation Adjusted Pension Income
   (Line 3 times Line 4)
     Husband _____ × _____
     Wife _____ × _____   _____

6. Annual Income from Social Security
   and Pension
   (Line 2 plus Line 5)   13,000
   Husband _____
   Wife _____

WORKSHEET VIII: FILLING THE GAP:
TOTAL SAVINGS NEEDED (cont.)

7. Additional Income Required
   (Line 1 minus Line 6)   22,000
   Husband _____
   Wife   _____

8. Retirement Income Factor—Table 9
   (Estimated Years in Retirement and Inflation
   Factor)
   Husband 15.37
   Wife   _____

9. Savings Required at Retirement Date
   (Line 7 times Line 8)   338,140
   Husband _____ × _____
   Wife   _____ × _____

the company does match it with half as much. She has about $5,000 in her 401(k), and another $8,000 in a rollover IRA from her job at the bank. The rest of her savings has gone into CDs and two mutual funds. Altogether, she has about $46,000. And she has paid cash for two more pieces of property with her friend—both on the island they will return to. One has a run-down house that they will demolish and replace with a two- or three-apartment home so they can live in one and gain income from the others.

Judy figures that living in the islands will be substantially cheaper, but that she will still need about $30,000 to $35,000 a year—mainly because she loves to travel.

Judy's worksheets show that she needs to save $11,935 annually to retire in 15 years. Can she do it? She says she can. Her income has gone up every year, and if she saves each increase, she may say farewell to the rat race before age 50! (She also expects that her half of the house, minus half of the mortgage, will provide money to help her in retirement, but she decided not to include this when figuring out how to fill the gap.)

WORKSHEET IX: FILLING THE GAP: SAVINGS NEEDED PER YEAR

1. Amount Already Saved on Tax-Deferred Basis
   Include amounts in IRAs, profit-sharing plans,
   401(k)s, Keoghs, SEPs, cash value of life insurance.
   Husband <u>13,000</u>
   Wife <u>   </u>

2. Value at Retirement (See Table 10: Estimated
   Rates of Return)
   (Estimated rate of return less inflation, based on
   years to retirement.)
   Husband <u>13,000</u> × <u>2.08</u> = <u>27,040</u>
   Wife <u>   </u> × <u>   </u> = <u>   </u>   <u>27,040</u>

3. Amounts Already Saved in Non-Tax-Deferred
   Investments
   Include amounts in savings, CDs, stocks, bonds,
   mutual funds, equity in rental real estate (not your
   principal residence).
   Husband <u>46,000</u>
   Wife <u>   </u>
   Joint <u>   </u>

4. Value at Retirement (See Table 10: Estimated
   Rates of Return times Line 4)
   (Estimated rate of return less inflation and income
   taxes, based on years to retirement.)
   Husband <u>46,000</u> × <u>1.56</u> = <u>71,760</u>
   Wife <u>   </u> × <u>   </u> = <u>   </u>
   Joint <u>   </u> × <u>   </u> = <u>   </u>   <u>71,760</u>

5. Amount Still Needed for Retirement
   Line 9 on Worksheet VIII minus   <u>239,340</u>
   Line 2 and Line 4
   Husband <u>   </u>
   Wife <u>   </u>

6. See Table 11: Assumed Discount Rate
   (Estimated rate of return less inflation [and taxes if

WORKSHEET IX: FILLING THE GAP:
SAVINGS NEEDED PER YEAR (cont.)

saving on after-tax basis], based on years to
retirement.)
   Husband ___·053___
   Wife   _____
7. Annual Savings Required for Retirement
   Line 6 times Line 5
   Husband 239,340 × __·053__ = _12,685_
   Wife   _____ × _____ = _____   12,685
8. Annual Employer Contribution to 401(k), Profit
   Sharing, ESOP, Etc.
   Husband _____
   Wife   _____   750
9. Annual Savings Needed
   Line 7 minus Line 8
   Husband _____
   Wife   _____   11,935

Jeanne and Matthew: Preparing to be Ready for
Whatever the Future May Bring

Jeanne and Matthew are both 35. They have a house, good jobs,
and a son who is a year and one-half old. Jeanne makes $60,000 a
year as a certified public accountant. Matthew earns $65,000 work-
ing in sales and marketing for a large corporation. They've been
married ten years—since they finished getting their graduate de-
grees.

During their first five years together, they rented an apartment
while they saved for the down-payment on a house. With the help
of both their parents, they paid $140,000 for a small three-bedroom
ranch—a house on a good lot in a comfortable family neighborhood,
and a house that promised easy adding on, either by finishing off
the upstairs or by expanding out in back.

Originally, Jeanne and Matthew considered their home simply as a starter. Like many of their friends, they expected to "move up." But now they see that conditions have changed. And they've seen how Jeanne's brother, James, has improved his house by remodeling it himself. They are thinking of remodeling their house. "We wouldn't dream of it if James didn't live so nearby," says Jeanne. "We'll be counting on his advice and skills."

But first they have to get their student loans paid off—probably by the end of next year—as well as their credit-card debt. Like many of their friends, they are paying now for the buy-now-pay-later frenzy of the 1980s—a syndrome that left them and so many others holding the bills for furniture, electronics, expensive vacations, and snazzy cars.

Two things combined to bring Jeanne and Matthew to their senses. One was the birth of their son, Taylor. The other was the realization that they were in the credit-card/student-loan crunch. "What really woke me up," says Matthew, "was when I was doing my income taxes a couple of years ago and I realized I couldn't deduct all those finance charges any more. I kind of smacked myself in the forehead and said, 'My God, that's just money down the drain!' "

Taylor's arrival added real emphasis to the need to rethink their money handling. "We just looked at the costs we added by having a baby," says Jeanne, "and we knew we had to change a lot of priorities." They simply put the credit cards away, she says, and now they have reduced the outstanding balances to the point where they should be entirely paid off within the next six months.

After the credit-card and student-loan debts are gone, they'll have only a car payment and the mortgage payment to face month in and month out. "Those we can handle," she says. "And we'll add onto the house slowly. That's something we have to do before we think about another baby."

Matthew has been mulling over their financial situation. "We never gave financial independence much thought before," he says. "But my dad got laid off last year. He was caught by what the experts like to call 'a corporate down-sizing.' Frankly, he was in no way prepared for that—emotionally or financially—even though he was getting along toward retirement age. Boy, he told us in no uncertain terms, 'Don't let this happen to you. Be prepared.' "

Matthew and Jeanne's financial planning has included life insurance. When they bought the house, they each took out a $100,000 term policy. They each doubled that when Taylor was born. At work, they each get double their salaries in term insurance the company pays for, so they feel they are well covered.

They're looking out for Taylor, too. When he was born, each grandfather put $1,000 into an aggressive growth fund for him, and they added $100 each on his first birthday. Meantime, Jeanne and Matthew have $50 withdrawn automatically from their checking account every month for transfer to the fund. Altogether, they figure on the account being worth $50,000 by the time Taylor is 18—maybe more, if the grandparents can continue to add to it each year. They know $50,000 won't be nearly enough for college by then, but, says Jeanne, "We both worked while we were undergraduates and graduate students, and we took out student loans, so Taylor can do the same."

As for 401(k) plans, Matthew has one at his workplace, but in the past he has never put in more than 2 percent. "I only did that because my dad insisted," says Matthew, "but I'll be upping that now." He plans to move to 6 percent—maybe as much as 10 percent—as soon as the student loans and credit cards are entirely out of the picture. His company will match with 3 percent. Jeanne, meanwhile, has a profit-sharing plan to which her company has contributed 10 percent of her salary each year. There is talk that the company plans to start a 401(k) plan soon. She will certainly contribute to it. Altogether, Matthew says, they will need to set aside at least $12,000 a year—and, even better, $15,000—in order to be financially independent by the time they are 55.

Jeanne went back to work a few months after Taylor was born, but her job is near home. She knows she could earn more by commuting into the city, but she doesn't want that hassle. They are now allocating part of their budget for child care. Matthew does commute, and travels around the country frequently for sales

WORKSHEET VIII: FILLING THE GAP:
TOTAL SAVINGS NEEDED

	Age Expected to Retire	Estimated Years in Retirement	Estimated Years to Retirement
Husband	55	25	20
Wife	55	30	20

Estimated Inflation Rate __4%__

Estimated Rate of Return __10%__

1. Desired Gross Annual Income
   (Use 70 to 80% of present income)
   Husband 45,500
   Wife   42,200   87,500

2. Estimated Annual Social Security Benefit
   (Amount you would receive if retiring this year)
   Husband 13,000
   Wife   13,000   26,000

3. Estimated Annual Income from Defined Benefit
   Plan(s) at Anticipated Retirement Date
   Husband 1 12,000   2 _____   12,000
   Wife   1 _____ 2 _____   _____

4. Inflation Adjustment Factor—Table 8
   (Inflation Adjustment for Pension without COLA)
   Husband __.624__
   Wife   _____

5. Inflation Adjusted Pension Income
   (Line 3 times Line 4)
   Husband 12,000 × .624
   Wife   _____ × _____   7488

6. Annual Income from Social Security
   and Pension
   (Line 2 plus Line 5)   33,488
   Husband 20,488
   Wife   13,000

WORKSHEET VIII: FILLING THE GAP:
TOTAL SAVINGS NEEDED (cont.)

7. Additional Income Required
   (Line 1 minus Line 6)   54,012
   Husband 45,500 - 20,488 = 25, 012
   Wife   42,000 - 13,000 = 29,000

8. Retirement Income Factor—Table 9
   (Estimated Years in Retirement and Inflation
   Factor)
   Husband 12.78
   Wife   13.78

9. Savings Required at Retirement Date
   (Line 7 times Line 8)
   Husband 25,012 × 12.78 = 319,653
   Wife   29,000 × 13.78 = 399,040   718,693

meetings. He has built a solid reputation and earned regular healthy increases in pay—not to mention recognition and tempting offers from competing companies. He figures his next move will bring a big jump in salary and benefits, but he is being extremely careful about considering offers.

What will they do when they kiss the rat race good-bye? They don't know yet. "But with what I've learned about marketing and selling, and with Jeanne's strong skills in accounting and in general business, there's almost nothing we couldn't do," says Matthew. "I really didn't think much about doing something else until my father got laid off. Now I've got to admit it—I've got a bee in my bonnet. I'm beginning to dream about all the things I'd really like to do. So is Jeanne. We're having a good time. We read about something, and when we both get excited we get carried away figuring out how we could do it better. Nowadays, I think of everything I learn as a stepping stone to something else."

WORKSHEET IX: FILLING THE GAP:
SAVINGS NEEDED PER YEAR

1. Amount Already Saved on Tax-Deferred Basis
Include amounts in IRAs, profit-sharing plans,
401(k)s, Keoghs, SEPs, cash value of life insurance.
   Husband _8,500_
   Wife _32,500_

2. Value at Retirement (See Table 10: Estimated
Rates of Return)
(Estimated rate of return less inflation, based on
years to retirement.)
   Husband _8,500_ × _3.21_ = _27,285_
   Wife _32,500_ × _3.21_ = _104,325_   _131,610_

3. Amounts Already Saved in Non-Tax-Deferred
Investments
Include amounts in savings, CDs, stocks, bonds,
mutual funds, equity in rental real estate (not your
principal residence).
   Husband _____
   Wife _____
   Joint _12,000_

4. Value at Retirement (See Table 10: Estimated
Rates of Return times Line 4)
(Estimated rate of return less inflation and income
taxes, based on years to retirement.)
   Husband _____ × _____ = _____
   Wife _____ × _____ = _____
   Joint _12,000_ × _1.81_ = _21,720_   _21,720_

5. Amount Still Needed for Retirement
Line 9 on Worksheet VIII minus
Line 2 and Line 4
   Husband _319,653 - 27,285 - 10,860* = 281,508_
   Wife _399,040 - 104,325 - 10,860* = 283,855_   _____

6. See Table 11: Assumed Discount Rate

   *one-half of 21,720 (line 4)

WORKSHEET IX: FILLING THE GAP:
SAVINGS NEEDED PER YEAR (cont.)

(Estimated rate of return less inflation (and taxes if saving on after-tax basis), based on years to retirement.)

Husband $\underline{.033}$

Wife $\underline{.033}$

7. Annual Savings Required for Retirement
   Line 6 times Line 5
   Husband $\underline{281,508}$ × $\underline{.033}$ = $\underline{9289}$
   Wife $\underline{293,855}$ × $\underline{.033}$ = $\underline{9367}$ $\qquad$ $\underline{18,656}$

8. Annual Employer Contribution to 401(k), Profit Sharing, ESOP, Etc.
   Husband $\underline{1950 - 3\%\ 401(k)}$
    profit
   Wife $\underline{6000\quad 10\%\quad sharing}$ $\qquad$ $\underline{7950}$

9. Annual Savings Needed
   Line 7 minus Line 8
   Husband $\underline{9289 - 1950 = 7339}$
   Wife $\underline{9367 - 6000 = 3367}$ $\qquad$ $\underline{10,706}$

Building a Second Career

Like Ken and Shelley, you may be thinking about early retirement as an opportunity to do something you've always dreamed about. If it's an income-producing business, you can use your second career to help fill the income gap until Social Security and a pension, if you have one, kick in as a source of income. But, first things first.

Can you do it? Once you've stepped off the treadmill, can you turn your skills to something entirely different from what you were doing before, or adapt them to a distinctly different version of your previous career? Can you become a magician, potter, writer, craftsman, pilot, landscape architect, or consultant—as some people described in this book have become?

Yes. Yes, yes, yes. You can. What you need to do is plan. And keep your vision clear. And dedicate yourself to making it happen.

Depending on the particular second career you have in mind, you may have to build up some skills, or develop new ones, during the years while you are still working at your present job. You will want to hone the hobbies that you are going to depend on later. Maybe take some night courses in adult education at your high school to learn some new angles. Build up your contacts and your network (as well as your net worth), keeping in mind the need to establish a strong reputation in your chosen field.

What do you *need* to get into your second career—in addition to your contacts, your network, and your reputation? Ken needed a potter's wheel; Danny a deck of cards, a top hat, and a bunch of large silk handkerchiefs; Eric a computer and a FAX machine (one of each in New Hampshire and in California, so he and his wife had only to carry floppy discs across the country); Ted a darkroom and all its equipment. So the start-up capital varied widely among them. But each had to invest in a telephone answering machine.

In many, many consulting and service businesses, you don't need to put up much capital to get started. Computer, FAX, phone, answering machine, copier—these basics can get most businesses under way. Office space? You may find an excellent deal in shared office space. Or you may find that setting up an office at home can work out just fine.

Financially, of course, you will have to know some basics about taxes and your business. As a self-employed person, you are required to file Schedule C with your income-tax return. You are allowed to deduct from your gross sales the cost of doing business. For Ken, this includes the cost of clay, travel and expenses at craft fairs, and advertising. For Ted, it includes the basic camera and darkroom equipment as well as film, printing paper, developer and hypo and other supplies. Since he maintains a studio at home, he can deduct a percentage of the expense of maintaining the house that applies to the studio.

WARNING: Home-office deductions are sticky. If you claim this deduction, the IRS is likely to take a close look at your return. Starting in 1992, it has even included a special form for the home-office deduction.

When you have deducted all such expenses, you wind up with a net income figure. The amount you must pay into Social Security and your federal income tax are both based on this net income figure. NOTE: You will find that you will now pay a higher Social Security tax because you yourself are both the employer and the employee—i.e., the company isn't there any more to make its contribution, for the company is now you.

One of the advantages you gain is that you may open a Keogh plan—a tax-deferred pension to which you are permitted to contribute a percentage of your net income.

IMPORTANT: Keep accurate records for your new business. Don't mix them with earlier records from, for instance, your free-lance work. Always be ready for the IRS audit you don't want.

Still Not Convinced You Can Do It?

But what if building a second career that produces a reliable income is not part of your game plan? What if you do not have a pension, or if you received a lump-sum settlement that you rolled over into an IRA, and you want to leave that alone until you reach 59½? How will you manage until you can make penalty-free distributions from rollover IRAs and Social Security benefits begin? Here's how some people managed:

• Eric and Valerie made a killing on their house. Sure, they sold it when the market was high, and they were able to buy another house not too long afterward, when the real estate market had become depressed. The fact is that, even if they had waited a couple of more years to sell, they still would have made a bundle, for they had paid $125,000 and added large amounts of sweat equity to bring their selling price up so high.

• Andy's plan is to roll his profit-sharing plan into an IRA, and keep it parked there until he's 59½. Meanwhile he will sell the company stock he has been buying regularly since he started work. In addition, he has been granted stock options, and will exercise them within the first few years after he officially retires. If he finds that he needs more money, he can take some out of his rollover IRA and pay the penalty and taxes, or annuitize it with monthly payments based on his life expectancy. As for his house, he will probably have to take a loss, but he will counterbalance that bad news by moving to another part of the country where living costs are much lower. There he will pay cash for a house and assume no mortgage. Since he is currently still working, he has not decided whether he will look for work after he gets off the full-time tread-mill. He is keeping his options open, knowing he won't be adverse to a part-time job.

• Lloyd and Frank both sold their businesses and started new ventures. Frank was already well supplied with tools for his handy-man service. Lloyd had to use some of his capital to set up his fruit-and-vegetable stand. Fortunately he had contacts, through his brother, in that business.

• And don't forget Nora and Howie. They started saving, on an after-tax basis, at the beginning of their marriage. They will tell you that they lived well during their working years—in a lovely house with a small mortgage and no other debts. Without ever being frivolous, they owned a boat and, later, an airplane. Now the income from their portfolio and their part-time work is more than enough to keep them going until Social Security kicks in. But the lesson here is that you need to start saving seriously as early as possible, especially if you don't have a pension to count on.

There's also an important lesson to be learned from Judy and her friend. They might expect their house to lose value, for they bought it at the top of the market. But in fact it has increased in value, mainly because they have not only maintained it well but have done major renovations and additions themselves. The lesson is to maintain what you've got in good shape, and make additions and improvements. That's better than trading houses upward, which gets you a bigger mortgage and increases your maintenance costs. Judy, incidentally, will have no pension when she leaves real estate sales, but she expects her sound saving pattern to continue right up until that time.

Reduced life-style? Yes, for some. But well worth it, they will all tell you, for the freedom and independence that have come with kissing the rat race good-bye. If you have the desire, the dedication, the creativity to make the bold farewell move, you will find it well worth it, too.

The secret is simple: Plan early. Stick with it.

Index